Check and test

Physical Education

Barry Hodgson

Published by BBC Worldwide Limited,
Woodlands, 80 Wood Lane, London W12 0TT

First published 2003

Reprinted 2005

Printed and bound by Sterling Press Ltd, UK.

Contents

Introduction   page 4

Performance

Skeletal system
01 Function   6
02 Bones   7
03 Types of joints   8
04 Synovial joints   9
05 Cartilage and ligaments   10
06 Types of body movement   11

Muscular system
07 Muscle types and structures   12
08 Muscle action   13
09 Muscle contraction   14
10 Levers   15

Cardiovascular system
11 Blood vessels and circulation   16
12 The heart   17
13 Blood   18
14 Effects of exercise   19

Respiratory system
15 Structure   20
16 Breathing action   21
17 Energy systems   22

Acquisition of skill
18 Types of skill   23
19 Practice and learning   24
20 Information processing   25
21 Motivation   26
22 Arousal and aggression   27
23 Goal setting   28
24 Personality   29

Physiological factors
25 Body types   30
26 Gender: physiology   31

Technology
27 Clothing   32
28 Facilities and sports surfaces   33
29 Equipment   34

Health-related fitness
30 Health-related fitness   35
31 Strength   36

Skill-related fitness
32 Skill-related fitness   37
33 Cardiovascular fitness tests   38
34 Strength tests   39
35 Flexibility and agility tests   40
36 Other fitness tests   41

Training
37 Principles of training   42
38 FITT and training zone   43
39 Seasonal planning   44
40 Session planning   45
41 Mental and anaerobic training   46
42 Aerobics   47
43 Aerobic training   48
44 Fartlek aerobic training   49
45 Weight training   50
46 Circuit training   51
47 Altitude training and plyometrics 52
48 Flexibility training   53

Drugs and sport
49 Stimulants and analgesics   54
50 Anabolic agents   55
51 Beta blockers, diuretics, peptide 56
       hormones and analogues
52 Smoking and alcohol   57

Diet and exercise
53 Food   58
54 Balanced diet   59
55 Diet and energy   60
56 Diet for sport   61

Participation

Social reasons

57 Leisure time   62
58 Vocation   63
59 School: the National Curriculum   64
60 School: examinations   65
61 School: extra-curricular activities and clubs   66
62 Excellence and Sportsmarks   67
63 Sports Colleges   68
64 Access and age   69
65 Ability and disability   70
66 Gender   71
67 Family, ethnicity and friends   72
68 Tradition and culture   73

External influences

69 Sports councils   74
70 Sports governing bodies   75
71 The BST and the YST   76
72 Sports club funding   77
73 Grants and the National Lottery   78
74 Sport sponsorship   79
75 Sport sponsors   80
76 Media   81
77 Television   82

Organisation and provision

78 Local authority provision   83
79 Private and commercial organisations   84
80 Sports clubs   85
81 International events   86
82 Hosting international events   87
83 Olympics   88
84 The UK Sports Institute   89
85 Amateur and professional   90

Health and safety

86 Risk assessment: environment   91
87 Risk assessment: activities   92

88 Preventing injury   93
89 Causes of injury   94
90 Health and hygiene   95

Types of injury and treatment

91 General treatment: RICE   96
92 Skin and muscle injuries   97
93 Ligament and tendon injuries   98
94 Joint injuries   99
95 Bone injuries   100
96 Hyperventilation, shock, hypothermia and hyperthermia   101
97 Asthma   102
98 Emergency treatment   103
99 Resuscitation   104
100 Roles in sporting activities   105

Answers   106

About GCSE Bitesize

GCSE Bitesize is a revision service designed to help you achieve success in the GCSE exams. There are books, television programmes and a website, which can be found at **www.bbc.co.uk/education/revision**. It's called *Bitesize* because it breaks revision into bite-sized chunks to make it easier to learn. *Check and Test* is the latest addition to the *Bitesize* revision service.

How to use this book

This book is divided into the 100 essential topics you need to know, so your revision is quick and simple. It provides a quick test for each bite-sized chunk so you can check that you know it!

Use this book to check your understanding of GCSE Physical Education. If you can prove to yourself that you're confident with these key ideas, you'll know that you're on track with your learning.

You can use this book to test yourself:

- during your GCSE course
- at the end of the course during revision.

As you revise, you can use *Check and Test* in several ways:

- as a summary of the essential information on each of the 100 topics to help you revise those areas
- to **check** your revision progress: **test** yourself to see how confident you are with each topic
- to keep track and plan your time: you can aim to check and test a set number of topics each time you revise, knowing how many you need to cover in total and how much time you've got.

GCSE Bitesize website

There's nothing like variety for making revision more interesting, and covering a topic from several different angles is an ideal way to make it stick in your head.

The GCSE *Bitesize* Revision website provides even more explanation and practice to help you revise. It can be found at:

www.bbc.co.uk/education/revision

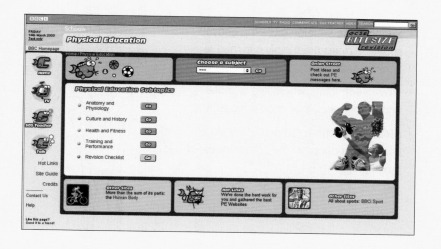

Skeletal system

Check the facts

> The skeletal system is the framework of the human body. It is made up of a range of different bones. The skeleton is held together by ligaments at the joints.

Four functions of the skeletal system

- **Protection:** many body parts are delicate and need to be protected against injury. The skull, or cranium, surrounds the brain; the vertebral column protects the spinal cord. The ribs protect the heart and lungs.

- **Support:** the skeleton gives the body its shape. Muscles are mainly attached to bones inside.

- **Movement:** joints, where two or more bones come together, enable movement.

- **Blood production:** red and white blood cells are produced in the bone marrow of long bones.

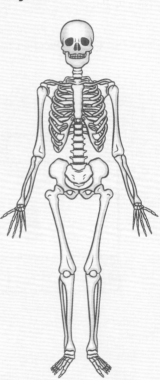

Test yourself

1 What are the four functions of the skeleton?

2 What are the most delicate parts of the body and how are they protected?

3 What is produced in the marrow of long bones?

Check the facts

There are 206 bones in the skeletal system. They are divided into four main types, each having a special function.

- **Long bones:** these are found in the arms, legs, ribs and collar bone. They are hollow, with bone marrow in the centre. Their structure provides strength but they are not very heavy.

Femur

- **Short bones:** short, squat bones found in the wrist (**carpals**) and ankles (**tarsals**). They are spongy with an outer layer of compact bone, making them light and strong.

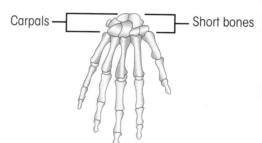

Carpals — Short bones

- **Flat bones:** plate-like bones, which form the skull, scapula and pelvis. Their large surface area provides good protection and attachment for muscles.

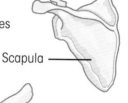

Scapula —

- **Irregular bones:** the vertebrae and small bones in the face are examples of irregular bones.

Vertebra —

Bone is formed from cartilage by a process known as **ossification**.

Test yourself

1 Name two important facts about the structure of long bones.

2 Where are short bones located?

3 Why are flat bones important?

Skeletal system

BBC GCSE Check and Test: Physical Education

Check the facts

**A joint is where two or more bones meet.
There are three classifications of joints.**

- **Fibrous:** no joint cavity but the bones are held together by fibrous tissue, e.g. in the case of the skull or the pelvis.

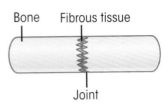

Fibrous joint

- **Cartilaginous:** no joint cavity, bones are connected by cartilage allowing some slight movement, e.g. the ribs to the sternum.

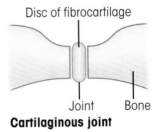

Cartilaginous joint

- **Synovial:** there are many different types of synovial joints, all of which have a joint capsule filled with synovial fluid.

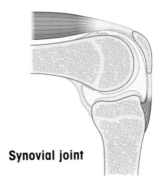

Synovial joint

Test yourself

1 Give two examples of where fibrous joints are located in the body.

2 Give one example of a cartilaginous joint and explain why there is restricted movement at this joint.

3 How do synovial joints differ from other joints?

Skeletal system

Check the facts

> Although synovial joints differ in shape and size, they all have similar characteristics. Each has a joint capsule filled with synovial fluid.

Six types of synovial joint

- **Ball and socket:** wide range of movement, e.g. the shoulder.

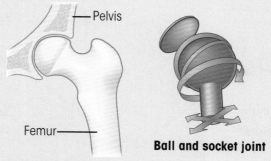

Pelvis

Femur

Ball and socket joint

- **Hinge:** movement in one plane, e.g. the knee.

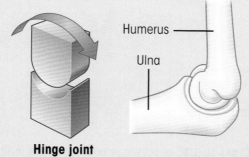

Humerus

Ulna

Hinge joint

- **Condyloid:** limited movement in two planes, e.g. the wrist.
- **Pivot:** limited rotation, e.g. the neck.
- **Saddle:** limited movement in two directions, e.g. the base of the thumb.
- **Gliding:** small range of movement, e.g. the vertebral column.

Test yourself

1 What are the two items found in all synovial joints?

2 Give one example of a hinge joint and explain how it's used in a sporting movement.

3 Where can you find a pivot joint and what is its purpose?

Skeletal system

BBC GCSE Check and Test: Physical Education

Check the facts

Articular cartilage is smooth and tough. It is found at the ends of long bones. It reduces friction and produces synovial fluid in the joint.

Fibro cartilage acts as a shock absorber between two bones in a joint. In the knee, it is sometimes called the **meniscus**.

Skeletal system

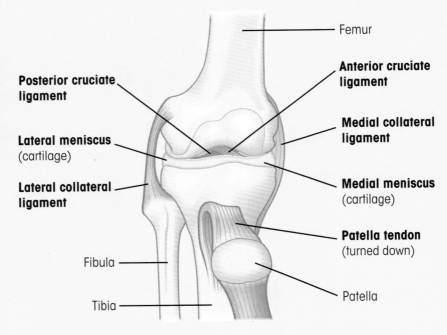

Femur

Anterior cruciate ligament

Posterior cruciate ligament

Medial collateral ligament

Lateral meniscus (cartilage)

Medial meniscus (cartilage)

Lateral collateral ligament

Patella tendon (turned down)

Fibula

Tibia

Patella

Cross section of cartilage and ligaments in the knee

Ligaments are strong connective tissues that hold the joint together. They are very complex in the knee joint.

Test yourself

1 What are the two types of cartilage and what is their function?

2 What are ligaments?

Check the facts

> Sporting movements are made up of a number of different types of body movement.

Six types of body movement

- **Abduction:** the limbs are moved away from the centre line of the body, e.g. moving the legs outwards when performing the splits in gymnastics.

- **Adduction:** the limbs are moved towards the centre line of the body, e.g. bringing the arms to the sides from an outstretched position.

- **Flexion:** bending at a joint, e.g. a bicep curl.

- **Extension:** straightening at a joint, e.g. kicking a ball in soccer.

- **Rotation:** the whole body is rotated, e.g. a somersault in trampolining.

- **Circumduction:** a limb making a rotational movement, e.g. bowling in cricket.

Test yourself

1 Give an example of a sporting activity where flexion and extension are continually repeated.

2 A trampolinist performs a 360 vertical turn and then a back somersault. Name the type of movement in both of these actions.

3 What type of movement is an ice skater doing when he or she is moving his or her arms inwards during a spin?

Check the facts

Muscular system

There are three main types of muscle.

- **Smooth** or involuntary muscle is found in the bowel and gut. It works automatically.

- **Cardiac** muscle is the specialised muscle of the heart. It contracts regularly and automatically. The speed of contraction can alter in response to drugs and stress. Adrenaline produced in the body can increase the heart rate.

- **Voluntary** muscle is also known as **skeletal** muscle. There are over 600 examples of this in the human body. Because of its composition, it is sometimes known as striated muscle.

Skeletal muscle is composed of fibres, which contract to produce movement.

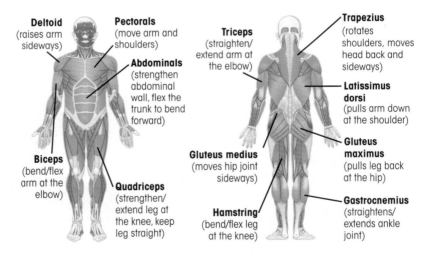

Deltoid (raises arm sideways)

Pectorals (move arm and shoulders)

Abdominals (strengthen abdominal wall, flex the trunk to bend forward)

Biceps (bend/flex arm at the elbow)

Quadriceps (strengthen/ extend leg at the knee, keep leg straight)

Triceps (straighten/ extend arm at the elbow)

Gluteus medius (moves hip joint sideways)

Hamstring (bend/flex leg at the knee)

Trapezius (rotates shoulders, moves head back and sideways)

Latissimus dorsi (pulls arm down at the shoulder)

Gluteus maximus (pulls leg back at the hip)

Gastrocnemius (straightens/ extends ankle joint)

There are two types of muscle fibres, fast and slow twitch.

Fast twitch fibres produce fast and powerful actions, such as sprinting, usually these are anaerobic activities. Aerobic activities, such as jogging and long distance running, rely more on **slow twitch fibres**.

Test yourself

1 Name the three types of muscle.

2 What happens when a muscle contracts?

3 In a triathlon, which types of muscle fibres are predominant in each of the three activities?

Check the facts

- Muscles never completely relax, there is always some **tension**.
- **Partial contraction** gives us muscle tone, which is important for good posture.

> **Sitting, standing, walking and carrying are everyday situations where muscles are working in conjunction with each other.**

Muscles often work in pairs, against each other. For instance, in the upper arm as the bicep contracts, the tricep relaxes and lengthens. The prime mover, the bicep, is known as the **agonist**. The tricep is the **antagonist**.

- The **synergists** or **fixators** stabilise the body position while other muscles are creating movement.
- **Tendons** attach muscles to the bone, at the origin and insertion.

This is shown in the diagram below.

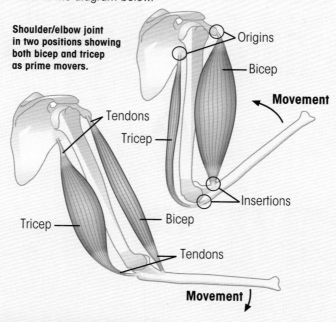

Shoulder/elbow joint in two positions showing both bicep and tricep as prime movers.

Origins
Bicep
Movement
Tendons
Tricep
Insertions
Tricep
Bicep
Tendons
Movement

Muscular system

Test yourself

1 How does muscle tone occur?

2 When using a bar to do a bicep curl, name the antagonist muscle and one muscle acting as a synergist.

3 What is a tendon? Name the two places where it is attached to a bone.

BBC GCSE Check and Test: Physical Education

Check the facts

There are three types of muscle contraction.

- **Isometric:** the muscle remains the same length throughout the action. Certain parts of the body need to be kept still while other parts are working. For example, in a bicep curl, the back and shoulder muscles are working isometrically to stabilise the body. This is known as synergist action. Pushing in a rugby scrum, when there is no movement, is also an example of isometric action.

- **Isokinetic:** the speed of movement remains the same throughout the action. When doing the butterfly stroke in swimming, the arms and legs are moving at relatively constant speeds.

- **Isotonic:** this muscle contraction can be subdivided into two types. **Concentric:** the muscle shortens as it contracts, e.g. lifting the bar in a bicep curl. **Eccentric:** the muscle lengthens, but under tension, e.g. lowering the bar in a bicep curl.

Test yourself

1 What are the three types of muscle contraction?

2 In rugby, how might isometric muscle contraction be used?

3 Using an example from athletics, explain how isotonic muscle contraction might be used.

Muscular system

www.bbc.co.uk/revision

Check the facts

To create movement, muscles contract and make use of different lever systems in the body.

- There are **three lever systems**, and each system has a **fulcrum** (turning point), a **load** (body weight or object) and an **effort** (a muscular force).

The diagrams below show the three lever systems, and how they create movement in the body.

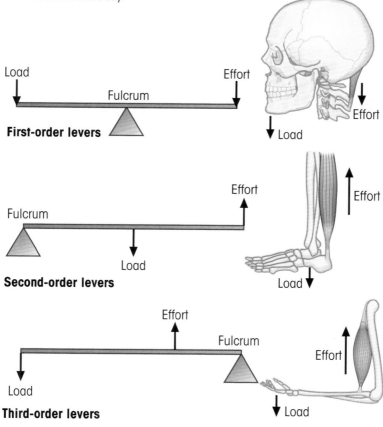

Load   Effort
Fulcrum
First-order levers

Effort
Load

Fulcrum   Effort
Effort
Load
Second-order levers
Load

Effort
Fulcrum
Effort
Load
Third-order levers
Load

Test yourself

1 Jumping in the air relies on the use of the gastrocnemius (calf) muscle. This is the force. What is the load and where is the fulcrum?

2 Draw a diagram to show the force, load and fulcrum when using a resistance machine to develop the quadriceps.

3 What is the lever system in a bicep curl and where is the fulcrum?

Muscular system

BBC GCSE Check and Test: Physical Education

Cardiovascular system

The cardiovascular system consists of the heart and blood vessels.

The **circulatory system** transports blood around the body, maintains body temperature and gives protection through antibodies (mainly in the white blood cells). Blood passes through tubes in the body, which are known as **blood vessels**.

Three types of blood vessels

- **Arteries:** mostly carry oxygenated blood away from the heart under pressure and into smaller tubes known as arterioles. The pulmonary artery carries de-oxygenated blood between heart and lungs.

- **Capillaries:** are tiny tubes, only one cell thick, that transport blood from the arteries to the veins. Food, oxygen, carbon dioxide and waste products are exchanged through their thin walls.

- **Veins:** carry blood back to the heart under low pressure. There are valves in the veins to prevent the blood flowing backwards and away from the heart.

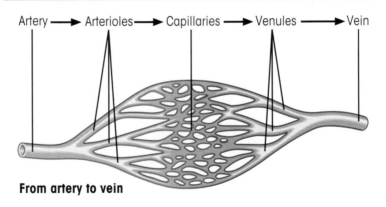

Artery → Arterioles → Capillaries → Venules → Vein

From artery to vein

Test yourself

1 What are the three functions of the circulatory system?

2 What are arteries, and what is special about the pulmonary artery?

3 What is the purpose of veins, and why do they have valves?

Check the facts

The heart pumps blood around the body through the blood vessels. The heart consists of four chambers.

The **right atrium** and **right ventricle** are linked by a **valve**. Similarly, the **left atrium** and **left ventricle** are also linked. The left and right sides of the heart are separated by the **septum**.

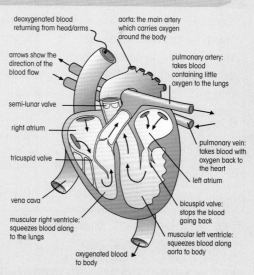

deoxygenated blood returning from head/arms

aorta: the main artery which carries oxygen around the body

arrows show the direction of the blood flow

pulmonary artery: takes blood containing little oxygen to the lungs

semi-lunar valve

right atrium

pulmonary vein: takes blood with oxygen back to the heart

tricuspid valve

left atrium

vena cava

bicuspid valve: stops the blood going back

muscular right ventricle: squeezes blood along to the lungs

muscular left ventricle: squeezes blood along aorta to body

oxygenated blood to body

Here's a simplified diagram of the heart and circulatory system:

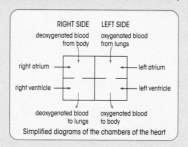

RIGHT SIDE   LEFT SIDE

deoxygenated blood from body   oxygenated blood from lungs

right atrium → ← left atrium

right ventricle → ← left ventricle

deoxygenated blood to lungs   oxygenated blood to body

Simplified diagrams of the chambers of the heart

Test yourself

1 What is the aorta?

2 Name one of the valves and explain its purpose.

3 Complete the simplified diagram of the heart.

Cardiovascular system

BBC GCSE Check and Test: Physical Education

Check the facts

Cardiovascular system

The composition of the blood

Red cells	White cells	Platelets	Plasma
Contain haemoglobin: a chemical compound of iron and protein. This combines with oxygen to become oxyhaemo-globin.	Contain phagocytes: pass through capillary walls and surround germs. Other white blood cells form antibodies that fight against germs and infection.	Fragments and particles that help clot the blood.	Mostly water, also amino acids, protein and glucose waste products.

The functions of the blood

Blood carries:

- oxygen from lungs to body cells
- carbon dioxide from body cells to lungs
- waste products and water from cells to kidneys
- glucose and nutrients from digestive system to cells
- hormones from glands to where they are needed
- white blood cells to sites of infection
- platelets to damaged capillary areas
- heat from warmer to cooler parts of the body.

Test yourself

1 What is the main function of red blood cells?

2 Which part of the blood carries:
  a oxygen
  b nutrients and waste products

3 How does the blood help combat infection?

Check the facts

> **The heart becomes more efficient as a result of EXERCISE.**

Training can increase the size and strength of the heart. This means that the pumping action becomes stronger and the size of the heart chambers increase, therefore, more blood can be pumped out!

Pulse is a measure of the heart rate. There are four types of pulse.

Name	radial	carotid	temporal	femoral
Location	wrist	neck	head	groin

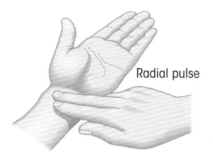

Radial pulse

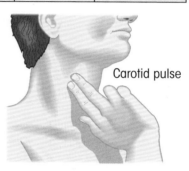

Carotid pulse

- **Stroke volume (SV):** the amount of blood leaving the ventricle on each heart beat.
- **Heart rate (HR):** the amount of blood pumped per minute.
- **Cardiac output (CO):** the stroke volume multiplied by the heart rate.

$$CO = SV \times HR$$

Test yourself

1 Where are the carotid and radial pulses taken?

2 What is meant by stroke volume and how does training affect it?

3 Two athletes have different heart rates and stroke volumes. Compare their cardiac output and indicate which athlete might have the more efficient heart.

    Athlete A: heart rate = 70 bpm, stroke volume = 70 ml

    Athlete B: heart rate = 90 bpm, stroke volume = 60 ml

Cardiovascular system

BBC GCSE Check and Test: Physical Education

Check the facts

Respiratory system

The respiratory system consists of:

- air passages
- the lungs
- the diaphragm

Air passes through the **larynx**, which is sometimes known as the voice box. Sound is produced by passing air over the vocal chords in the larynx.

Air is taken into the body through the **mouth** and **nasal cavity**. In the nostrils, the air is filtered by tiny hair (**cilia**), warmed, and moistened by **mucus**.

At the top of the throat is a flap of skin, the **epiglottis**, which prevents food or other particles entering the lungs.

The **trachea** is a large, flexible but strong tube, also known as the windpipe. Rings of cartilage maintain its shape.

The trachea branches into two to enter the lungs as **bronchi**.

Lung

The bronchus in each lung divides into **bronchioles**.

Vein

Bronchioles sub-divide into small air sacs, **alveoli**. Most of the lung tissue is made up of millions of alveoli, which is where the exchange of oxygen *into* the blood and carbon dioxide *out* of the blood occurs.

Venule

Alveoli

The alveoli are covered with very small vessels, **capillaries**, which allow oxygen and carbon dioxide to pass to and from the bloodstream.

Arteriole

Artery

Respiratory system

Test yourself

1 Name the three components of the respiratory system.

2 What is the purpose of hairs in the nose?

3 What is the function of the epiglottis?

4 What is the structure of the trachea and what is its common name?

5 Where are gases exchanged in the lungs?

Check the facts

There are two phases in breathing:

Breathing in

During **inhalation**, the rib cage moves upwards and outwards, while the diaphragm contracts, becoming flattened rather than dome shaped.

Inhalation results in an increase in volume of the thorax with a decrease in pressure compared with **atmospheric pressure** so that air rushes into the lungs.

Breathing out

During **exhalation**, the rib cage moves downwards and inwards, the diaphragm relaxes and becomes dome shaped and the air is forced out due to an increase in pressure helped by the recoil of the elastic lungs.

Respiratory system

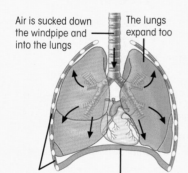

Lungs   Breathing in   Breathing out

Air is sucked down the windpipe and into the lungs

The lungs expand too

Lungs are compressed, pushing air out of the lungs and up to the windpipe

Intercostal muscles contract, pulling the rib cage upwards

As the chest expands, the diaphragm contracts. This pulls it down and makes the chest larger

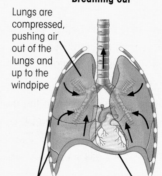

Intercostal muscles relax, lowering the rib cage and making the chest smaller

As the chest is made smaller, the diaphragm relaxes, making the chest even smaller

Key terms

- **vital capacity:** maximum amount of air breathed out in one breath
- **residual volume:** amount of air left in lungs after breathing out
- **respiratory rate:** breaths per minute
- **tidal volume:** amount of air taken in and out with each breath
- **minute volume:** amount of air breathed per minute

Test yourself

1 Where are the intercostal muscles and what is their purpose?

2 Where are oxygen and carbon dioxide exchanged in the lungs?

3 What is the relationship between minute volume, respiratory rate and tidal volume?

Check the facts

Respiratory system

> **Muscles need energy to work.**

Anaerobic (without oxygen)

1 Anaerobic: creatine phosphate system

- Creatine phosphate (CP) in the muscles combines with ADP to create ATP and this then releases energy.

> **CP + ADP = ATP = ADP + energy**

2 Anaerobic: lactic acid system

- When the creatine phosphate has been used up, the lactic acid system starts. ADP is combined with glycogen (GL) which produces more ATP and pyruvic acid.

> **GL + ADP = ATP + pyruvic acid**
> **pyruvic acid + oxygen = lactic acid**

- When there is a build up of lactic acid, muscles become painful and difficult to contract. To convert lactic acid back to pyruvic acid, oxygen is needed. If this is not available, then oxygen debt occurs.

Aerobic (with oxygen)

- Breathing supplies oxygen to the muscles and energy needs are met for continuous activities. Glycogen is processed to release energy.

> **GL + ADP = ATP + pyruvic acid**
> **pyruvic acid + oxygen = water + carbon dioxide + heat**
> **glucose + oxygen = energy + carbon dioxide + water**

Aerobic and anaerobic activities

- Different activities might use one or both of these energy systems. In team games where players are moving continually, they are using the aerobic system to provide energy. A short burst of speed, needing high amounts of energy, relies on the anaerobic systems, when lactic acid builds up in the muscles.

Test yourself

1 Briefly describe the differences between aerobic and anaerobic energy systems.

2 How does lactic acid affect performance and how is lactic acid removed from the muscles?

3 Name three activities where aerobic, anaerobic, and both energy systems are used.

Check the facts

> **Physical skills associated with sports are often known as motor skills.**

In some games, some skills are similar and, therefore, there is **positive transfer**, e.g. kicking a ball in soccer and rugby. However, skills in one game might have an adverse affect on another game. This is **negative transfer**. For instance, the follow-through with a tennis racket might not be safe on a squash court.

Skills can be classified under three headings

Open and closed

- **Open:** invasion games, such as rugby and netball
- **Closed:** diving, tennis serve

Pacing

- **External pacing:** a starting gun in athletics
- **Self-pacing:** taking a golf shot

Serial

- **Continuous:** swimming or running
- **Discrete:** clear start and finish, such as a somersault in gymnastics

Test yourself

1 Give one example of negative transfer and one example of positive transfer in an invasion game.

2 Put the following skills on the continuum line below.

tennis serve, tennis volley, hockey dribble, springboard diving

OPEN--CLOSED

3 a Give two examples of externally paced skills.
b Give two examples of discrete skills.

Acquisition of skill

BBC GCSE Check and Test: Physical Education

Check the facts

Acquisition of skill

> **To learn a new skill or improve an existing one, you must PRACTISE PRACTISE PRACTISE PRACTISE PRACTISE.**

- **Part method:** one way of learning a complex skill is to learn parts of it and then put the parts together, for example, when learning how to do the triple jump.

- **Whole method:** sometime the skill cannot be broken down easily, for example, when learning how to somersault.

- **Massed practice:** continual practice repeating the action over and over again, for example, when learning shooting or passing skills.

- **Spaced practice:** in strenuous events, the performer might need to rest either during the practice or between practice sessions, for example, when weight lifting or marathon running.

COACHING COACHING COACHING COACHING COACHING

Visual guidance	Verbal guidance	Manual guidance
Learn by watching a demonstration of the skill, looking at a picture or watching a video.	Learn by listening to instructions.	Learn by being helped with the support of a coach, by holding the performer in a position or with the use of a mechanical device, such as a rig in trampolining.

Test yourself

1 a Name two sports where massed practice is best.
  b Name two sports where spaced practice is best.

2 What might be the best form of visual guidance and why have you selected it?

3 Name two specific forms of manual guidance.

Check the facts

The diagram below shows a **model of information processing** when learning a skill.

Input

- Information comes into the brain through the senses, usually as visual information.

Decision-making

- Information overload: if there is too much information, then the brain has to reduce this.
- Limited-channel capacity: too much information is reduced because only a limited amount can be processed at one time.
- Selective attention: making sense of the information by perception and memory, so that only useful information is acted on.

Output

- The action resulting from the decision made.

Feedback

- As a result of the action in the output phase, the brain receives further information, which then contributes to the input.

Test yourself

1 What is limited-channel capacity?

2 Why is selective attention important?

3 Using a specific skill from a sport, explain the information processing system.

Acquisition of skill

BBC GCSE Check and Test: Physical Education

Acquisition of skill

Check the facts

Learning will only take place if the subject is **motivated**.

> **Motivation is the driving force that compels people to do something.**

People are motivated by different things; for some, it is **money**, for others, it is just **taking part** in an event.

Two main types of motivation

- **Intrinsic motivation:** taking part in a sporting activity is sufficient to motivate a person. This could be something like the London Marathon, or joining an aerobics class. However, in both these activities there could be other reasons, perhaps raising money for a charity in one and developing personal fitness in the other.

- **Extrinsic motivation:** taking part in an activity because of external factors, such as prize money or awards. For professionals, the motivation is financial – they play to earn money. However, there are many examples of non-financial rewards, such as trophies, medals, swimming certificates, which can be powerful motivators for school children. Even professional sportsmen and women may take part in a sport for the prestige, for example, in the Olympic Games, there is no prize money, only medals.

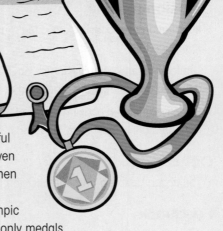

Test yourself

1 What is the usual type of motivation for an amateur sportsperson?

2 Give two examples of extrinsic motivation.

3 How might motivation change from intrinsic to extrinsic as a person gets older?

www.bbc.co.uk/revision

Check the facts

Arousal

> There are different levels of arousal in sport, but too little means involvement might be low, too much might lead to loss of control.

- A long jumper needs high arousal levels before starting their run up.

- A rifle shooter needs to be calm, with low arousal levels before shooting.

- A player in an invasion game may have to raise and lower arousal levels throughout the game.

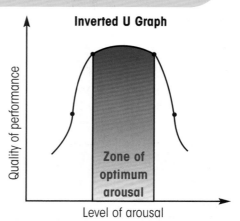

Inverted U Graph

Quality of performance

Zone of optimum arousal

Level of arousal

Aggression

> Controlled aggression is necessary in most sports.

- There is a need to be forceful and assert authority, particularly in team games such as rugby, or batting and bowling in cricket. A bowler may show aggression in bowling bouncers.

- In athletics, there may be aggression in the run up to a long or triple jump. The expression of 'attacking the board' is often used.

- However, aggression must be controlled, and when sportsmen and women lose this control it can often lead to foul play in many invasion games, as well as in games such as tennis where racket abuse sometimes occurs.

Test yourself

1 Give examples from sport where high and low levels of arousal are beneficial.

2 What is meant by controlled aggression?

3 What can happen when control of aggression is lost? Give examples.

Acquisition of skill

Check the facts

Setting personal goals is important. It might be to improve a personal best in an athletic event, or play a sport for your country.

> **A well-known system for target or goal setting is the SMARTER system.**

- **S**-pecific and focused.
  A time, distance or performance?

- **M**-easurable: assessed to show progress.
  Was the target achieved?

- **A**-ccepted: agreed between performer and coach.
  Communication?

- **R**-ealistic: achieveable goals.
  Too hard?

- **T**-ime: targets to be reached at specific times.
  Next event, next year?

- **E**-xciting: targets challenging and rewarding.
  Maintain motivation?

- **R**-ecorded targets: written, so that progress can be judged.
  Checklist?

Test yourself

1 Describe what is meant by the SMARTER system.

2 How might the 'M' be used in target setting for an athletic event?

3 If the target set for the performer is too hard, which part of the SMARTER system should be applied?

Check the facts

People have different personalities. Do sportsmen and women take part in a sport because of their **personality profile**, or does the sport itself affect their personalities?

Two main types of personalities

INTROVERTS quiet, shy and retiring	EXTROVERTS outgoing, loud, lively
PREFERRED SPORTS	
Individual sports – gymnastics Intricate skills – fencing Restricted movements – archery Routine and repetitive – swimming	Team sports – hockey Whole body activities – diving Lots of movement – tennis High levels of excitement – skiing

Test yourself

1 Give examples of two sportspersons that take part in individual sports who may be introverts.

2 Give three reasons why extroverts might prefer invasion games, and give an example of one sportsperson who might be considered an extrovert.

Check the facts

W. H. Sheldon classified people by three body types:

Mesomorph	**Ectomorph**	**Endomorph**

broad shoulders	narrow shoulders	narrow shoulders
narrow hips	narrow hips	wide hips
muscular	little muscle	lots of body fat
low body fat	little body fat	

Everyone is a mix of all three types!

- Sportsmen often have particular **body types**, which are advantageous for their sport.

In gymnastics, having good muscular strength in relation to body size is an advantage and, therefore, many gymnasts are likely to be meso/ectomorphs. In events where objects are thrown, such as shot and discus, athletes tend to be a mix of meso/endomorphs.

- **Height** and **weight** are also important factors in some sporting activities.

Being tall is an advantage in basketball, but not in gymnastics. In rugby, forwards tend to be heavier than backs.

- **Body composition**

Two people of the same weight may have different proportions of fat, muscle, bone and connective tissues. The amount of body fat can be measured using skin-fold callipers.

Test yourself

1 Name two sporting events where players are always of a similar size and weight.

2 Give two examples of sports which might be suitable for:

a A meso/ectomorph

b A meso/endomorph

3 Name one team sport where there are a variety of body types. Give specific positions associated with different body types.

Check the facts

Fewer females take part in sport than males.

- There are many reasons for this (see topic 66), but one of these could be **physiological**. Some sports have been considered too dangerous for women. In the 1928 Olympics, some women collapsed during the 800 metre race. After this, the event was withdrawn and it was not until the Rome Olympics in 1960 that the event was reinstated for women.

- Four events – the 3000 metre steeplechase, hammer throw, triple jump and pole vault – were not open to women until after the triple jump was introduced into the women's athletics competition at the Atlanta Olympics in 1996.

- Female competitors have yet to match the performances of males in athletic events, and there are few events where males and females compete against each other. In some sports and activities, the rules forbid having mixed competitions, often on the grounds of **safety**. Boys and girls are not allowed to play in competitive football matches in mixed teams over the age of 11.

However, the number of women in sport is increasing all the time.

- Football has become popular at both school and club level for female competitors. Rugby is developing for women and female boxing competitions are now a regular feature in the sporting press.

Test yourself

1 Name one sporting event where women do not compete.

2 Name two athletic events that were not open to women until recently.

3 Name two sports where men and women compete against each other directly.

Physiological factors

BBC GCSE Check and Test: Physical Education

Check the facts

New materials and new designs of equipment have had a considerable impact on sport.

Technology

- **Clothing:** new materials and designs for **one-piece suits** for swimming, speed skating and athletics have contributed to improved performance times in these and similar events. Clothing for outdoor activities has changed considerably over the years. New **lightweight windproof** and **waterproof** materials provide very good protection for walkers and climbers in extreme conditions. Fabrics such as Gore-tex® provide good protection but also allow the body to breathe and, therefore, reduce the build up of sweat. Kevlar®, developed for body protection in the Armed Forces, is now extensively used in cricket and hockey.

- **Footwear:** sports companies spend considerable amounts of money developing different types of footwear, not just to improve sportsmen and women's performances, but also to maintain sales in the fashion and recreational market. **Air-cushioned soles** in training shoes, plastic ski-boots, and sports shoes for specific events in athletics are some of the developments that have taken place with sports footwear.

Test yourself

1 How have the material and design of sports clothing changed in recent years?

2 What effect has this had on performances in two sporting events?

3 Name one sport and the material which has been used to increase competitors' safety in the sport.

Check the facts

Facilities

> **New facilities now enable events to take place which would previously have been cancelled because of weather conditions.**

- The Millenium Stadium in Cardiff with a **retractable roof** allows football, rugby, and cricket to take place irrespective of bad weather, and in Australia, the roof of the national tennis stadium can be closed when the weather is too hot.

> **Large stadia are multi-purpose, and adapted for different sporting events.**

Sports surfaces

- New surfaces, such as **plastic grass**, have revolutionised the way hockey is played. Artificial cricket wickets are popular in schools, as they require considerably less maintainance than traditional grass wickets. Some football clubs installed artificial pitches, but these were replaced by grass because not all clubs were able to practise and play on this type of surface.

- Times and distances have improved in athletics with the introduction of **rubberised surfaces**, and **soft landing areas** for high jump and pole vaulting make these events safer for athletes.

- There is a wide variety of indoor sports surfaces, from wood and carpet vinyl to block tiles. **Sprung floors** reduce impact stress in events, particularly in gymnastics.

Test yourself

1 Give two advantages of having a retractable roof on a stadium.

2 Some sports governing bodies are against playing on artificial surfaces. Name one of these and the reason why.

3 Name one game where the introduction of artificial surfaces has revolutionised the game, with two examples of improvements to the game.

Technology

BBC GCSE Check and Test: Physical Education

Technology

Check the facts

> New technology has been applied to
> a variety of sports equipment.

Four areas influenced by new technology

- **Performance:** artificial surfaces for hockey have led to better control in receiving and passing, and this has increased the speed of the game. **Fibre glass** poles for pole vaulting have led to a significant improvement in heights cleared. In javelin, the design has been altered to increase the distances thrown. In racket games, the use of **graphite** has produced stronger and more powerful rackets.

- **Teaching and coaching: video recording** of a sport is useful for the coach and the performer, to analyse technique and make comparisons with top class performers. Heart monitors help coaches set training levels. Analysis of movement in individual and team games using a **computer** can help coaches improve individual technique and patterns of team play.

- **Refereeing: video replay** is now used in a number of sports to help the referee make decisions. In swimming and athletics, **electronic starting, timing** and the use of **photo finishing** help officials make the correct decisions. The **electronic eye** in tennis can be used to detect whether a service is in.

- **Spectators:** at the back of a large stadium, spectators have little chance of seeing the action. However, large **video screens** show replays, and **miniature cameras** in cricket stumps give spectators a taste of what batsmen expect from fast bowlers.

Test yourself

1 Some performances have been improved by the introduction of sports equipment with new designs and materials. Give two examples of this.

2 Give two examples of how new technology has affected:

a coaching and teaching

b spectators.

Check the facts

> Fitness is a measure of the body's ability to complete activities for everyday life efficiently and effectively.

Four measures of fitness

- **Cardiovascular endurance:** sometimes known as stamina. It is the ability of the heart to pump blood and deliver oxygen where needed in the body. Cardiorespiratory endurance includes heart, blood vessels, lungs and the respiratory system.

- **Muscular endurance:** the ability of the muscles to contract over a relatively long period of time without tiring. This is important for activities such as walking, running or swimming.

- **Speed:** the ability to move the body and limbs quickly, as in running fast or throwing a ball in cricket or rounders.

- **Flexibility:** the range of movement at the joints. This is important as it reduces muscle injury and allows for a full range of movement. It is essential for events such as hurdling, gymnastics and swimming.

Test yourself

1 Define fitness.

2 a What is meant by cardiovascular endurance or stamina?

  b Give two examples from a sport where cardiovascular endurance is important.

3 Name two sports where muscle endurance is necessary and name the muscle areas involved.

4 Name two sports, with specific reference to areas of the body, where flexibility is important.

Check the facts

Three types of strength

- **Dynamic:** required to start and maintain movement of the body, e.g. starting a sprint race and then maintaining the effort until full speed is reached.
- **Explosive:** required when a high amount of force has to be applied quickly, e.g. shot putting.
- **Static:** required when applying strength to a fixed or static object, e.g. pulling in a tug of war or pushing in a rugby scrum.

Power is a combination of strength and speed.

Test yourself

1 What is explosive strength and in which two athletic events might it be important?

2 What is power?

3 Complete the table below.

Sport	Type of strength: Dynamic, Explosive or Static	Activity
Rugby	Static	
Badminton		Smash
Gymnastics		Somersault
Swimming		
Netball		
Cricket		

Check the facts

Five components of skill-related fitness

- **Agility:** the ability to change body direction quickly and accurately.

- **Balance:**

  static – holding a position without movement, e.g. a handstand

  dynamic – maintaining a position when moving, e.g. cycling or surfing.

- **Coordination:** putting actions involving the limbs and the whole body together, e.g. pole vaulting.

- **Reactions:**

  simple – responding to a signal, e.g. sprint start to a gun

  choice – responding to a variety of signals, e.g. playing a shot in cricket.

- **Timing:** performing an action or movement at the exact time, e.g. heading a ball in soccer from a corner.

Test yourself

1 Name two sporting activities where agility is important.

2 Balance is important for many sporting activities. Give examples of static and dynamic balance.

3 How do simple and choice reactions differ? Give examples to illustrate your answer.

Skill-related fitness

BBC GCSE Check and Test: Physical Education

Skill-related fitness

Check the facts

Three cardiovascular fitness tests

The Harvard step test

This tests how quickly a person recovers (returns to a normal pulse rate).

Procedure:
- take resting pulse rate twice – record lowest score
- step up and down on a platform 50 cm high
- step for five minutes at the rate of 30 steps per minute
- take pulse rate at one minute intervals for three minutes after five minutes of stepping
- use formula and tables provided to score fitness levels.

The Cooper 12-minute run

This tests aerobic capacity or VO_2 max (the maximum amount of oxygen used).

Procedure:
- warm up thoroughly
- walk or run as many laps of a marked distance as possible
- record the distance run after 12 minutes
- use table provided to score fitness levels.

The multi-stage fitness test

Procedure:
- warm up thoroughly
- using a firm surface with lines 20 metres apart, run between the lines at a pace set by the tape provided
- time allowed between levels decreases and, therefore, pace of running is increased
- record the level reached (25 levels maximum)
- use table provided to score fitness levels.

Test yourself

1 How does the recovery rate of a person relate to their fitness levels?

2 Describe in detail one aerobic capacity or VO_2 max test.

Check the facts

Three strength tests

Sit-up test

Measures muscular endurance.

Procedure:
- subject lies on mat, knees at right angles and arms across chest
- ankles held by partner or fixed under wall bars
- sit-ups done in specific time with the tape provided
- frequency increased
- score recorded and tables provided used to determine fitness levels.

Sergeant jump (vertical jump)

Measures explosive strength.

Procedure:
- subject stands facing wall, both feet touching, and stretches hands as high as possible
- height marked on wall
- subject stands sideways and jumps and touches wall as high as possible
- distance between two marks measured
- best score of three recorded and table used to determine standard.

Standing broad jump

Measures explosive strength.

Procedure:
- subject stands behind line marked on mat
- two-footed standing take-off and landing as far along the mat as possible
- distance jumped is marked; if subject falls back, then no jump
- best score of three recorded and table used to determine standard.

Test yourself

1 What is meant by muscular endurance and how might it be tested?

2 The vertical and standing broad jumps are both tests of explosive strength. Suggest why one might be easier than the other. Remember to describe the test procedure of your selected test.

Skill-related fitness

BBC GCSE Check and Test: Physical Education

Check the facts

Skill-related fitness

Flexibility and agility tests

Sit and reach test

Measures flexibility at the hip joint, which is generally restricted by the hamstrings.

Procedure:
• thorough warm up with stretching exercises
• bare feet placed against the edge of a box
• using a metre rule, subject stretches as far forward as possible with hands
• record best of three attempts and use table to determine standard.

Illinois agility run

Procedure:
• thorough warm up
• subject completes a marked course as quickly as possible
• record better of two attempts and use table to determine standard.

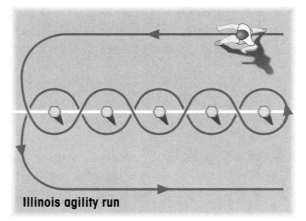

Illinois agility run

Test yourself

1 Flexibility at the hip and shoulder are essential for many sports. Describe one test of flexibility at one of these joints.

2 The Illinois run involves complicated instructions and a specially laid out circuit. Devise a simpler test for general agility.

Check the facts

Balance, coordination and reaction-time tests

Stork stand

Tests static balance.

Procedure:
• subject stands on one leg with foot of other leg against support leg
• record the length of time balance is held
• attempt balance using either leg.

Alternate hand ball throw

Tests hand-eye coordination.

Procedure:
• subject stands two metres away from wall
• tennis ball is thrown with one hand and caught with the other
• number of successful catches made in 30 seconds.

Ruler drop

Simple reaction-time test.

Procedure:
• subject rests hand on edge of table, with thumb and forefinger extended
• ruler held by partner between subject's thumb and finger at specified height above
• without warning, ruler is dropped and subject catches it as soon as possible
• record best of two attempts with each hand.

Double ruler drop

Choice reaction-time test.

Procedure:
• as above, but using two hands and two rulers
• record best of two attempts and add distances.

Test yourself

1 The stork stand is a test for static balance. Can you devise a test for dynamic balance? (Refer to topic 32.)

2 Devise a test for foot coordination using the alternate hand ball throw test.

Skill-related fitness

BBC GCSE Check and Test: Physical Education

Check the facts

Training needs to be done to maintain or improve fitness levels and skilled performances.

Four basic principles of training

- **Specificity:** training must be specific to a particular sport or aspect of fitness.
- **Overload:** overloading body systems with higher work rates and increased loads means the body has to adapt and meet these demands. This can be done in three ways:

  frequency – number of training sessions, e.g. one per week or per day.

  intensity – increasing distances run, repetitions or weight.

  duration – length of training sessions.

- **Progression:** as the body adapts, training needs to be more progressive so that greater demands are made. It is a necessary progression from simple skills through intermediate to complex skills. Sometimes the performer makes little progress and reaches a plateau where performances remain the same, but this may be only for a short time.

- **Reversibility:** use it or lose it. The body also adapts to reduced levels of training, particularly fitness training, although well-learned skills are not lost in the same way.

Test yourself

1 Give two reasons why training is necessary.

2 What is meant by reversibility?

3 Overload is important in training. Name the three ways this can be achieved and illustrate your answer making use of training in a specific sport or activity.

Training

www.bbc.co.uk/revision

Check the facts

Frequency	Intensity	Time	Type
How often?	How hard?	How long?	What kind?

To stay FIT, use FITT.

Training zone

- The intensity of training is very important; too little and the body does not need to adapt, too much and the body cannot adapt.

- A safe training zone depends on the age and fitness levels of the subject. The maximum safe level is known as the **threshold**.

This can be worked out using the following formula:

> **220 – age of subject = maximum heart rate**

Examples:

1 For a student aged 15, $220 - 15 = 205$, so 205 is the maximum heart rate.

2 For an adult aged 40, $220 - 40 = 180$, so 180 is the maximum heart rate.

- The older the subject, the lower the maximum heart rate!

- The training zone is normally between 60–80 % of the maximum heart rate.

This is shown in the graph below.

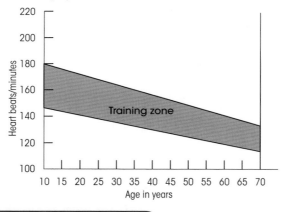

Test yourself

1 Show how you would apply the FITT principle to training in your sport.

2 a What is the maximum safe heart rate for a 20-year-old?

   b How does the maximum heart rate change with age?

3 Sketch a graph of the training zone using the vertical axis for heart rate and the horizontal axis for age.

Training

BBC GCSE Check and Test: Physical Education

Training

Check the facts

Long-term planning

- Most sports men and women plan their training for a particular event or season. However, many sports now have longer seasons because of better indoor facilities.

- Some athletic events are held throughout the year. In rugby, players could take part in rugby union in the winter months and rugby league in the summer.

- Some sportsmen and women target specific times when they expect to be at their best for a special event, perhaps a World Championship or Olympic Games. This is known as **peaking**.

Seasonal-training programme

- **Out of season:** this usually includes light training, maintenance of fitness levels, and taking part in another sport to prevent staleness.

- **Pre-season:** an increase in the intensity of training; improve and refine skills in preparation for the season.

- **Early season:** take part in selected events, improve fitness levels, maintain skills work, mental preparation and physical rest before competitions.

- **Peak season:** regular competitions with appropriate rest periods between them. During peak season, an athlete will maintain fitness levels, mental preparation, diet and exercise prior to competitions.

Test yourself

1 Long-term planning is important for performers in all sports, however, because of the increase in indoor events and world-class competitions, top-class performers are now involved throughout the year.

   a Name two sports where performers compete throughout the year.

   b Name two sports which are seasonal, one in the winter and one in the summer.

2 **a** How might a performer prevent becoming bored with his or her sport out of season?

   b In the early part of a season, what might a performer do to prevent injury and prepare for more regular competitions in the peak season?

www.bbc.co.uk/revision

Check the facts

A single training session is often split up into a range of different activities.

Warm up

Fitness training

Skills training

Cool down

- **Warm up:** preparing the body for exercise accomplishes three things. It increases the blood flow to the muscles, stretches muscles and tendons and increases mental arousal.

- **Fitness training:** many sports require high levels of aerobic fitness and, therefore, exercise to improve cardiovascular fitness will be the focus. However, in some activities, anaerobic fitness or flexibility may be the specific aspect to be developed.

- **Skills training:** individual and team skills need to be practised, e.g. place kicking in rugby or shooting in netball. Small groups practise improving team skills, such as penalty corners in hockey. An athlete may also have pressure training in specific skills. Team and unit skills are practised using passive and then active opposition.

- **Cool down:** training sessions should finish with warm-up exercises, but less vigorous than in the warm up. This prevents blood pooling in the legs.

Test yourself

1 a Give three reasons for warming up at the start of a training session.

   b Why should some warm-up activities be used at the end of a training session?

2 Making use of your chosen sport, explain pressure training in detail.

3 In learning a new skill, why is it important to start with passive opposition and then progress to active opposition?

Training

BBC GCSE Check and Test: Physical Education

Check the facts

Mental training

> **Mental stress on top-level sportsmen and women is high.**

- Some sports governing bodies employ sports **psychologists** to help performers set goals and targets for future competitions and help them come to terms with previous defeats.

Effects:
- Raises self-esteem and helps the athlete focus on targets.

Advantages:
- Helps performers to cope with high stress levels and previous defeats.

Disadvantage:
- The performer may find it hard to discuss issues with a psychologist.

Anaerobic training

> **Short bursts of activity are required in many sports.**

- Examples of this type of activity are a run-up for a vault in gymnastics or a sprint in rounders. Training is done by **repetitions** of short sprints (10–20 metres), or short bursts of activity under 10 seconds duration.

Effects:
- The heart walls (particularly in the left ventricle) grow stronger and pump more blood.
- There is a faster dispersal of lactic acid enabling longer muscle action.

Advantages:
- These are specific to each sport.

Disadvantage:
- There is little variety in training method.

Test yourself

1 What might a sports psychologist discuss with:

  a An individual sportsman or women?

  b A team player?

2 a What activities need good anaerobic fitness?

  b Name two effects of anaerobic training.

Check the facts

Aerobics classes

> **This is usually continuous movement done to music, using the arms, the legs and the whole body.**

Some of the variations are:

Step classes	Aquaerobics	Chair aerobics
Aerobic routines carried out making use of a small platform, which increases the intensity of some exercises.	Aerobics performed in a swimming pool. Water provides resistance and, therefore, intensity. However, water also provides buoyancy and relieves stress on the joints.	An effective way of maintaining fitness for older people and wheelchair users.

Effects of aerobic classes:

- heart becomes more efficient
- stroke volume is increased and heart rate is lowered
- recovery to normal heart rate is quicker
- blood volume, red cells and haemoglobin levels increase
- arteries grow larger
- diaphragm grows stronger
- lungs expand more, increasing volume
- alveoli (air sacs that make up the lung tissue) become more efficient.

Test yourself

1 Aerobic classes have been modified in a number of ways.

   a Explain what is meant by step aerobics.

   b What are the advantages of aquaerobics?

2 Explain how aerobic training affects:

   a the cardiovascular system

   b the respiratory system.

Training

BBC GCSE Check and Test: Physical Education

Training

Check the facts

Interval training

> Intermittent **training at a high intensity interspersed with rest periods is called interval training.**

- Specific times and distances are set – 30 metres plus, from 30 seconds up to five minutes. During rest periods, the body is able to recover from oxygen debt. Needs to be well planned and is often used in athletics and swimming.

Advantages

- Distances and times can be adapted for individual performers.
- Suitable for a variety of sports and targets can be easily set.
- Can be used for aerobic or anaerobic fitness or a mixture of both.

Disadvantages

- Needs careful and accurate planning.
- Can be repetitive and boring.

Continuous training (long/slow distance)

> **Working without rest can only be done with** moderate intensity, **usually at 75% of maximum intensity, but fitter performers can work at a higher rate.**

- Continuous exercises, such as jogging, swimming as well as aerobic type classes, maintain high heart rates over sustained periods of time.

Advantages

- Requires little equipment, easy to organise.
- Training levels can be easily controlled by the performer.

Disadvantages

- Does not develop anaerobic fitness.
- Difficult to accurately measure training amounts.
- Can be monotonous.

Test yourself

1 At which point during interval training is oxygen debt repaid?

2 Which sports make use of interval training, and what might be the minimum distances and times used?

3 Give two advantages and two disadvantages of continuous training.

Check the facts

Fartlek

Fartlek is a Swedish training method meaning speed play.

- There are no specific distances and times for the different types of activity – based on how the performer feels. Both aerobic and anaerobic training can take place.

A typical session could be:

- 5 minutes slow jog
- 3 minutes normal jog
- 3 minutes fast walk
- 5 minutes fast jog
- 2 minutes hopping on alternate legs
- 5 minutes 30 metre sprint
- 3 minutes fast jog
- 2 minutes fast walk
- 2 minutes cool down

Advantages

- Range of both aerobic and anaerobic training.
- Can be adapted for different sports, variety of activity.
- Needs little special equipment.

Disadvantages

- Difficult to measure training amounts.
- Needs self-discipline to maintain work rates.
- Not sport specific.

Test yourself

1 What does the Swedish word 'fartlek' mean?

2 Give two specific examples from Fartlek training, times or distances, in which both aerobic and anaerobic training can take place.

3 Give one advantage and one disadvantage of Fartlek training.

Training

BBC GCSE Check and Test: Physical Education

Check the facts

> **Weight training is an effective way of improving muscle strength.**

- **Muscular endurance:** use a light weight with many repetitions.
- **Explosive strength:** use a medium weight and move very fast.
- **Static strength:** use a heavy weight with few repetitions.

Weight training machines have now replaced free weights in schools and sports centres. Some of the advantages are:

- they are safer and more comfortable to use
- they work specific muscle groups
- the amount of weight used can be easily adjusted
- they can be used in a small space effectively
- they can help with motivation as the weight lifted can be seen easily.

Repetitions: the number of times a weight is lifted.

Sets: the number of times the activity is repeated in a training session.

Training and muscle action

- **Isometric:** use very heavy weights with little or no movement.
- **Isokinetic:** weights provide resistance through the full range of movement.
- **Isotonic:** muscle shortens (concentric contraction) or lengthens (eccentric contraction) as the weight is being lifted.

Advantages

- Specific muscle groups can be targeted.
- Can be used for most sports.
- Muscle strength and endurance can be effectively increased.

Disadvantages

- Special equipment needed which may be expensive.
- Needs special location to be used safely.
- Needs to be well planned with correct techniques.

Test yourself

1 Give three reasons why weight machines are better than free weights.

2 What is the general principle to increase muscular endurance?

3 Explain the difference between isometric and isotonic training, using either free weights or a machine.

Training

Check the facts

Circuit training is an **adaptable** form of training. A **variety of exercises and skills** are done at different locations in a gym or hall, known as **stations**.

**Circuits can be designed for fitness,
skills or a mixture of both.**

Planning a circuit

When planning a circuit, you need to consider the following things:

- purpose of the circuit (e.g. skills, fitness) and type of activities to be used
- number of stations in the circuit and number of circuits altogether
- time on each activity and time of the entire training session
- number of repetitions and rest or recovery time.

Example of a nine station circuit to improve cardiovascular fitness

sit ups (abdominals)	bench dips (arms)	step ups (legs)	squat thrust (abdominals and legs)	press ups (arms)
star jumps (legs)	pull ups (arms)	burpees (abdominals)	shuttle run (legs)	

Advantages

- Variety of activities which help maintain motivation levels.
- Adaptable for a variety of sports for fitness and skills.
- Can be done with little specialist equipment and a large number of people in a small area.
- Can incorporate aerobic, anaerobic and weight training exercises.

Disadvantages

- Needs considerable organisation and planning.
- May need some specialist gym equipment.

Test yourself

1 Plan a skills circuit for an invasion game of your choice.

2 Give six examples of exercises that might be included in a general cardiovascular fitness circuit.

3 Name four advantages of circuit training.

Training

BBC GCSE Check and Test: Physical Education

Check the facts

Altitude training

In preparation for the Olympic Games in Mexico City (altitude 3000 m), many countries used **high altitude** training centres to help their athletes prepare for the event. Training at high altitude is particularly important for middle and long distance runners. At altitudes where there is less oxygen available, the body increases the mass of red blood cells along with haemoglobin levels. When the athletes compete at lower altitudes, they use the **increased levels of oxygen** more effectively and so often improve on their performances.

Advantages

- Very effective for events requiring high aerobic fitness levels.
- Good preparation for events at both high and low altitude.

Disadvantage

- Expensive for countries without high mountains.

Plyometrics

A training method to improve **explosive strength**. Based on **jumping type activities**, muscles are rapidly stretched and the energy generated in the elastic part of the muscle is used to rebound. **Endurance** and **static strength** are also increased using this method.

Advantages

- Little specialist equipment required.
- Can be used for different sports.

Disadvantages

- Not suitable for inexperienced sportsmen and women.
- Training levels cannot be measured easily.

Test yourself

1 What is the effect of high altitude training on the body, and why is it suitable training for low altitude competitions?

2 What is the main disadvantage of altitude training?

3 a What is plyometric training?

   b Which aspect of fitness is developed using this method?

Training

Check the facts

Maintaining and improving flexibility, with a good range of movement at the joints, is an essential component of fitness.

This enables muscles to work more effectively. In javelin throwing, the range of movement at the shoulder joint determines how long force can be applied to the javelin. Repeated short actions, such as kicking a football, can restrict movement at the hips as the hamstrings may shorten. There are four ways of improving flexibility.

Static stretching

- A muscle is held in a stretched position for a short time. As flexibility increases the time can be extended, but it should be at least 10 seconds. The subject is in full control of this type of stretching.

Passive stretching

- An external force is applied to a joint. This is usually done by a partner or coach. However, care must be taken as the subject does not control this stretching.

Active stretching

- Sometimes known as ballistic stretching, this is done by moving the limbs vigorously. Although effective, warm up must be extensive to reduce the risk of injury.

PNF stretching (Proprioceptive Neuromuscular Facilitation)

- Immediately after contracting, muscles can be more easily stretched. The muscle is contracted against a high resistance, and then immediately stretched to its full range.

Test yourself

1 In some sports, flexibility at certain joints is essential for good performances. Name two of these sports, giving specific examples of why flexibility is important.

2 What is ballistic stretching and what needs to be done to minimise the risk of injury?

3 Why might passive stretching be both very effective but also dangerous?

Training

BBC GCSE Check and Test: Physical Education

Drugs and sport

Check the facts

In 1994, the International Olympic Committee (IOC) categorised all sports-related drugs.

Stimulants

- These **raise the heart rate** and **stimulate the nervous system**. Reactions are improved and the person feels more alert, with increased confidence in their abilities. High levels of work can be maintained without the feeling of pain and fatigue.

Examples	Side effects
• **caffeine**, which is found in coffee and tea • **amphetamines** – ephedrine, dexedrine, benzedrine and 'speed'	• increase in hostility • high blood pressure • irregular heart beats • overheating of body as pain and fatigue signals are suppressed • mental depression • addiction

Narcotic analgesics

- These **suppress pain** and enable athletes to continue to perform when injured. After a hard physical performance they **encourage sleep**, enabling the body to recover. Narcotics cause drowsiness and analgesics are pain-killers.

Examples	Side effects
• **morphine** – medical pain-killer • **heroin** – medical pain-killer • **codeine** – available over the counter as a pain-killer and is sometimes found in medicines for diarrhoea	• highly addictive • constipation • mental apathy • low blood pressure • over training when injured

Test yourself

www.bbc.co.uk/revision

1 What stimulant is found in tea and coffee?

2 Give two examples of stimulants and suggest why a sportsperson might take this type of drug.

3 Name one narcotic analgesic and give three of its side effects.

Check the facts

Anabolic agents

- Commonly known as **anabolic steroids**, these are developed artificially to perform the same function as hormones, specifically, the male hormone testosterone, which is responsible for the development of male characteristics, such as a deep voice, hair on the chin and muscle growth.

In most sports, muscular power and endurance are important. Anabolic steroids **increase the rate of muscle growth** and **raise competitiveness**.

Examples	Side effects
• nandrolone • stanozolol • artificial testosterone • clenbuterol	• heart disease • high blood pressure • bone, tendon and ligament weakness • infertility • growth of facial hair in females • deepening of voice in females • liver disorders • balding in females • acne • stunted growth in children • aggressive behaviour

Test yourself

1 What is the male hormone and what is its effect?

2 a What are the perceived benefits of taking anabolic steroids?

   b Name two events where performers may have an advantage over other competitors by taking anabolic steroids.

3 Give six side effects of taking anabolic steroids.

Drugs and sport

BBC GCSE Check and Test: Physical Education

Check the facts

Drugs and sport

Beta blockers

- To perform some sports well, it is necessary to **lower anxiety levels** either before or during the event. Rifle shooting and snooker are two of these sports. Beta blockers **slow down heart and breathing rates**.

Examples	Side effects
• propranolol	• drowsiness
	• insomnia
	• mental depression

Tranquillisers, such as diazepam (valium), are also used to reduce anxiety levels. They cause **muscle relaxation** and are **addictive**.

Diuretics

- In events such as boxing, wrestling and judo, getting the right body weight just before the event is important. Diuretics increase the amount of water in the urine, which not only **reduces body weight quickly**, but may also **disguise traces of drugs in the urine** by diluting it.

Examples	Side effects
• furosemide	• rashes
• probenecid	• nausea
	• loss of sodium and potassium salts
	• muscle weakness and numbness

Peptide hormones and analogues

- These are growth hormones, which **control pain** and increase the amount of red blood cells.

Examples	Side effects
• corticotrophin	• increased risk of strokes
• gonadotrophin	• abnormal growth
• erythropoietin (EPO)	

Test yourself

1 Name two sports where it is advantageous to lower the heart rate before or during the event. What drugs are used to do this?

2 Why would diuretics be used and in what type of sporting event?

Check the facts

Smoking

Nicotine is taken into the blood stream through smoking. It is an **addictive** drug, which raises the heart rate and blood pressure.

There are other ways smoking can damage health:

- lung cancer – tars are deposited in the lungs, making them less efficient and can lead to cancer
- increased risk of heart disease
- carbon monoxide reduces the effectiveness of the oxygen-carrying capacity of haemoglobin
- throat cancer
- reduced levels of fitness
- less resistance to illness, such as bronchitis
- loss of smell, taste and appetite
- passive smoking affects other people.

Alcohol

Small quantities of alcohol are not harmful to general health, but it does affect performance in sport. Alcohol contains the chemical **ethanol**, which acts on the brain. Further effects:

- balance, co-ordination and reactions are affected
- diuretic – alcohol can increase water levels in urine and cause dehydration
- loss of body heat – increased blood flow to skin causes loss of heat
- reduction of glycogen levels and slower lactic acid removal
- judgement affected, leading to accidents
- aggressive behaviour.

Recreational drugs, such as barbituates, cocaine, cannabis or LSD (as well as amphetamines and heroin), are illegal and addictive. Some can have fatal consequences. They have no place in sport.

Test yourself

1 How does smoking affect the respiratory system, and why might this cause reduced performance levels in sport?

2 Give examples of the long term effects smoking can have on a person.

3 Name two ways in which excessive alcohol consumption affects physical performance.

Drugs and sport

BBC GCSE Check and Test: Physical Education

Diet and exercise

Check the facts

Food is the body's source of energy. Diet is important, not only to maintain healthy body systems, but also to provide energy for exercise.

- **Carbohydrates:** the body breaks down carbohydrates to provide **glucose** and **glycogen**. Carbohydrates can be split into two types. **Simple** carbohydrates are known as sugars, e.g. in jam, honey, cakes, chocolate, fruit, milk and sugar. **Complex** carbohydrates are known as starches, e.g. in vegetables, cereals, rice, pasta and bread. During digestion, carbohydrates are broken down into glucose. Glucose is converted into glycogen and stored in the liver and muscles.

- **Fats:** energy can be provided by fats but is not as readily available as energy from carbohydrates. **Saturated fats** are found in animal products like milk, meat, cheese, cream and butter. **Polyunsaturates** are found in fish and vegetable oils. Fatty animal products contain **cholesterol**. Too much cholesterol in the blood leads to a clogging of the artery walls increasing blood pressure and causing circulatory problems.

- **Proteins:** made from **amino acids** and essential in building cells, making blood and regenerating muscle tissue. Amino acids are contained in meat, fish, eggs and cheese.

- **Vitamins: trace substances** in food, which are necessary for the normal efficient functioning of the body. One of their roles is to regulate chemical reactions in the body.

- **Minerals:** very small quantities of **chemical substances** in food. Calcium in milk; iron in meat, liver and green vegetables are examples of minerals.

- **Fibre:** found in wholemeal bread, vegetables, fruit and cereals. Fibre **does not contain nutrients** but provides bulk for food and is **essential to digestion**.

- **Water:** makes up **two thirds of the body's contents**.

Test yourself

1 Give examples of simple and complex carbohydrates.

2 Carbohydrate is broken down into glucose. What is it converted into then and where is it stored in the body?

3 What is cholesterol and why is it harmful?

www.bbc.co.uk/revision

Check the facts

The body needs to take in the correct proportions of different foods, so that essential elements are included.

A good balanced diet should look something like this:

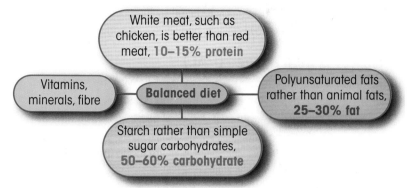

White meat, such as chicken, is better than red meat, **10–15% protein**

Vitamins, minerals, fibre

Balanced diet

Polyunsaturated fats rather than animal fats, **25–30% fat**

Starch rather than simple sugar carbohydrates, **50–60% carbohydrate**

Additives

- Most packaged foods contain additives that enhance flavour and colour the food. They have no nutritional value, and some people have allergies to some additives. Food packaging in the UK has to list any E-numbers, identifying the additives.

Dietary problems

- Having too much or too little of one type of food or the wrong type of food can lead to dietary problems. Eating more food than is required will cause an increase in weight, as the body will store up the excess as fat. If this is excessive, then **obesity** occurs. Insufficient food intake is also a health risk and this can occur when a person suffers from **anorexia**, a mental illness affecting the appetite.

Dieting

- Dieting, by reducing the amount of food eaten, may reduce weight, but does not necessarily reduce the fat content of the body.

Test yourself

1 What is meant by a balanced diet and what does it consist of?

2 What is the purpose of additives in packaged food?

3 Name two eating disorders and explain them.

Diet and exercise

BBC GCSE Check and Test: Physical Education

Diet and exercise

Check the facts

> Food provides energy. Different amounts of
> energy are necessary for different activities.

Basal metabolic rate (BMR)

- This is the **lowest level** of energy required by the body for normal healthy living and is determined by age, sex, body size and body composition.

Physical activity level (PAL)

- The amount of energy required to perform an activity. The higher the activity level, the higher the energy input and output needed.

> The total energy needed = BMR + PAL

- Energy is measured in **joules** or **kilojoules**, typical examples of energy needed each day are shown in the table below:

Age and activity	Male	Female
8 years	8 200 kJ	7 300 kJ
15 years	11 500 kJ	8 800 kJ
adult office worker	10 500 kJ	9 000 kJ
adult manual worker	14 000 kJ	10 500 kJ
retired adult	9 000 kJ	7 000 kJ

Test yourself

1 What is meant by BMR?

2 In general, why do females have lower energy requirements than males?

3 Why might a male adult office worker require less energy than a 15-year-old male per day?

Check the facts

Sports with high activity levels need considerable amounts of energy.

Much of this energy will come from **glycogen** stored in the muscles. There is a limited amount, but it can be increased by eating extra carbohydrates, which are then converted into glycogen. Energy is also taken from **fat** stored in the body during aerobic exercise when there is plenty of oxygen available to release energy from fat.

Activity	Energy used/hr	Activity	Energy used/hr
rugby	1 130 kJ	walking	380 kJ
squash	1 254 kJ	golf	560 kJ
jogging	1 320 kJ	badminton	710 kJ
cycling	1 380 kJ	tennis	1 000 kJs
swimming	1 500 kJ		

Before exercise

• A planned diet is essential. In events, such as boxing or judo, where weight is critical, diet must be exact. Sportspersons involved in long-distance events need to increase the amount of carbohydrate they eat. **Carbohydrate loading** will increase the amount of glycogen available. Eating immediately before an event is unwise as the digestive system requires increased blood supply and a full stomach will put further strain on the abdominal muscles. A light meal two hours before the event should include starches, but not simple sugars, as they increase insulin levels and can lead to tiredness.

During exercise

• **Fluids** need to be taken during extended activities, such as marathons and long-distance cycling, to prevent dehydration. Drinks containing glucose are beneficial as they help conserve glycogen stores.

After exercise

• **Isotonic drinks** help with rehydration and restoration of glycogen levels.

Test yourself

1 Why are carbohydrates important in energy production?

2 Why would competitors go to a 'Pasta Party' the day before a marathon?

3 What is the purpose of an isotonic drink after exercise?

Diet and exercise

BBC GCSE Check and Test: Physical Education

Social reasons

Check the facts

Leisure time is non-working time.

> **For many people, sporting activity, either as a player or spectator is an essential part of their leisure time.**

Changes in working patterns have led to increased leisure time. Before the industrial revolution, leisure time would have been restricted to saints' days, festivals and public holidays. When people started to work in factories, they had much less leisure time, but as technology developed, the working day became shorter and workers gained more time for leisure.

Factors leading to an increase in leisure time

Work patterns

• Not everyone employed works the traditional full day. Many more people work part-time or flexi-time (starting or finishing at atypical times) than before. More and more people are able to work from home.

Unemployment

• People may be unemployed for many reasons: a lack of job opportunities in their area; seasonal work or redundancy.

Early retirement

• Increasing numbers of people are able to retire early – well before 60 or 65. These people may still wish to pursue an active lifestyle. Many may take up new leisure activities such as golf, hill walking or other outdoor pursuits.

Technology

• This has had an impact in the work place and the home. Production lines with computer-controlled equipment require fewer people. Office work can be done at home through computer links. At home, labour-saving devices, such as washing machines and dishwashers, have significantly reduced the time it takes to do household tasks.

Test yourself

1 Give a brief definition of leisure time.

2 How have work patterns led to an increase in time available for leisure?

3 How has technology at work and home affected time for leisure?

www.bbc.co.uk/revision

Check the facts

Amateurs

- The majority of sportsmen and women are amateurs, but not all who take part in sport do so entirely for recreational purposes. International competitors need to train and compete all year round and their sport can become practically a full-time job. Before many sports became professional and semi-professional, competitors would receive sponsorship to cover expenses, training costs, and equipment. Some of these sportsmen and women may have employers who would give them time off to train and compete, and continue to pay their salaries.

Semi-professionals

- Some sportsmen and women earn money from their sport, but it may not be sufficient to live on and, therefore, they may have some other employment as well. These sportspersons are known as semi-professionals. There are many semi-professionals in different sports today. The most popular semi-professional sport is, and has always been, football.

Professionals

- Many people now take part in sport as full-time professionals. At one time, football, rugby league, cricket and boxing were the only professional sports in the UK. With the relaxation of amateur rules in many sports, there has been a considerable growth in professional sport. At all levels of sport, professionals are now involved. Local league cricket might employ a professional who will play and coach. International athletes can no longer take part in world sporting events as either amateurs or semi-professionals.

(See topic 85 for more information about amateur and professional issues.)

Test yourself

1 What is the difference between a professional and a semi-professional sportsperson?

2 Name two sports that have had professional players for many years.

3 What is the most popular semi-professional sport in the UK?

Social reasons

BBC GCSE Check and Test: Physical Education

Social reasons

Check the facts

Schools, both public and state, continue to have a considerable influence on participation in sport.

The National Curriculum and Physical Education

In September 2000, a new National Curriculum was introduced into state schools. This means that students, irrespective of where they live, should have similar experiences in Physical Education. Students are allocated to different **Key Stages** depending on their age. For each Key Stage, a Physical Education curriculum has been decided as laid out in the table below.

Key Stage	Students Age	Year Group	Activities in Physical Education
1	5–7 yrs	1–2	Games, gymnastic activities and dance
2	7–11 yrs	3–6	Games, gymnastic activities, dance, athletic activities, outdoor and adventurous activities, and swimming. Students taught all six areas of activity.
3	11–14 yrs	7–9	Students taught four of the above activities.
4	14–16 yrs	10–11	Students taught a minimum of two of the above activities; one must be a game.

This means that the Physical Education programme of every school will have some similarities. Because each school has **different facilities**, they are allowed to choose the activity areas which are most appropriate for their school.

There is no national curriculum in Physical Education for **students over 16** years of age. Most schools offer examination and recreational courses for these students.

Test yourself

1 What is the purpose of having a National Curriculum for Physical Education?

2 Name four of the six areas of the National Curriculum for Physical Education taught at Key Stage 2.

3 Why might there be some variations in the Physical Education curriculum at different schools?

www.bbc.co.uk/revision

Check the facts

Examinations in Physical Education

At Key Stage 4 and at A level, students can take examinations in Physical Education. At Key Stage 4, age 14–16, these are **GCSE** exams organised by examination boards. Students can take courses in either Physical Education or Games and they are **assessed on practical activities** as well as the **written examinations**. Because some schools cannot allocate sufficient time for students to take the full GCSE courses, examination boards now provide a range of **short courses**, which still have both written and practical elements.

Students doing their **A levels**, aged over 16, can take more advanced examinations in Physical Education; Advanced Subsidiary in the first year and Advanced (A2) in the second year. Although there are **practical elements** to these advanced courses, students have to learn **much more** about the **theory** of the subject than for GCSE. These qualifications are useful for students wishing to take degrees in subjects such as sports science, recreation management and the teaching of Physical Education.

Some schools and colleges offer Key Stage 4 and A level students a range of **General National Vocational Qualification** (GNVQ) courses, such as Leisure and Tourism or Sport and Recreation, which have some Physical Education elements.

Some schools offer **Junior Sports Leader Awards** for students at Key Stage 4 and **Community Sports Leader Awards** for students at A levels.

Test yourself

1 What are the two main elements of GCSE Physical Education courses?

2 What examinations, apart from GCSE, can students take in Key Stage 4?

3 What examinations are usually available to A level students and what value do they have?

Social reasons

BBC GCSE Check and Test: Physical Education

Social reasons

Check the facts

Schools and colleges usually provide a range of opportunities to take part in sporting activities in addition to those of the National Curriculum.

These are known as **extra-curricular activities** because they take place outside of normal school time, usually at lunchtime, before and after school or at weekends. Extra-curricular activities often include **interschool fixtures**, which are important as they help develop high standards and help talented students to have the chance to play for their city, county or country.

Factors determining extra-curricular activities

- the activities included in the school Physical Education curriculum
- the facilities available to the school
- the interests and skills of the teachers
- the involvement of local clubs and coaches and parents

In nearly all sports, there is a natural progression from school to international sport.

There are schools national governing bodies, such as the **English Schools Athletics Association** and the **English Schools Football Association**.

School and local sports clubs

Links between schools and local sports clubs benefit both the school and the club. Many talented students may play for local sports clubs. Some clubs may make use of school facilities for their training and matches. Schools can provide clubs with a constant source of members, whilst clubs might help schools with the provision of facilities and coaching.

Test yourself

1 What is meant by the term 'extra-curricular activities'?

2 Why are these important for students who are talented in sporting events?

3 Give two reasons that might determine the range of extra-curricular sporting activities.

4 What advantages are there for a school with close ties to a local sports club?

Check the facts

Raising the Game

In 1995, the Conservative Government launched 'Raising the Game' which has four aims:

- to put sport at the heart of weekly life in every school
- to improve the provision of sports facilities
- to provide a better link between school and club sport
- to develop sporting excellence.

Sportsmark and Sportsmark Gold awards

Secondary schools (and colleges) can bid for these awards. The following information is used to decide whether a school should get these awards.

- **Curriculum:** does the school curriculum follow the National Curriculum? Curriculum activities must be of 12 hours in length (i.e. six hours of athletics in Year 7 and six hours in Year 8).
- **Extra-curricular activities:** twelve opportunities for activity for all students; four recreational activities or clubs and eight competitive activities, such as interform or interschool events.
- **Sportsmark:** 35% of students should be taking part in extra-curricular activities.
- **Sportsmark Gold:** 50% of students should be taking part in extra-curricular activities.
- **Leadership:** students should experience leadership inside and outside of lessons.
- **Sporting partnerships:** the school should have partnerships with sports clubs, leisure centres, other schools or youth groups.
- **Professional development for teachers:** there must be evidence of teachers continuing training in all aspects of Physical Education.

Activemark and Activemark Gold

This is an award similar to 'Sportsmark' but for primary schools. It was started in 2000.

Test yourself

1 What are two of the aims of 'Raising the Game' and how do these affect participation in sport?

2 Give two standards that a school has to meet to gain a 'Sportsmark'.

3 Why might a school not be considered for a 'Sportsmark Gold'?

Social reasons

Check the facts

In 1996, the Conservative Government launched the **Sports College scheme**.

> **Schools and colleges can apply to become Sports Colleges if they meet certain criteria.**

Objectives of the scheme:

- to award students a sports qualification such as GCSE Physical Education or the equivalent

- to increase the range and take up of sports, courses and qualifications for students

- to maintain Physical Education and sports courses for post-16 students

- to increase the time available for Physical Education by increasing the length of the school day

- to identify and develop sporting potential for gifted children

- to develop links with governing bodies of sport

- to expand the schools facilities and encourage wider community use.

Schools applying for the scheme have to prove their ability to meet these demands and are expected to:

- have good sporting facilities

- have a 'Sportsmark' award

- have raised £50 000, which is matched by the government.

The **Youth Sport Trust** working with the **Department for Education and Skills** is responsible for deciding which schools become Sport Colleges.

Test yourself

1 What are four of the objectives of the Sports College scheme?

2 What organisations decide on the status of Sports Colleges?

Check the facts

Many factors affect participation in sport.

Access

> There are many providers of sports facilities, but participation may be restricted because specific facilities may not be available in the area or cannot be reached easily.

Most rural and urban areas have multi-purpose sports centres and are able to provide for a wide range of sports. However, provision for **high-level performers** in gymnastics, diving, ice skating and other events **may be restricted to large urban areas**. Access to sports centres may be more difficult in rural areas because of distances and lack of public transport.

Age

> The sport and leisure that people take part in is often closely related to their age and local traditions.

As people get older, not only do they take part in less sport, but **the nature of sport changes** too. Taking part in gymnastics when young is ideal, when the body is flexible. In contact sports, such as soccer and rugby, the recovery time is longer as people age. Swimming competitively is mostly associated with young people but this does not stop older people from enjoying swimming.

> Some activities are suitable for all ages because skill rather than strength, speed and power are more important.

Golf is a good example. Walking, green bowling and swimming are some of the other activities enjoyed by all ages, but particularly older people.

Test yourself

1 Why might participation in certain sports for high-level performers be restricted?

2 Name two sporting activities that are suitable for people of all ages.

3 Why might invasion games be unsuitable for older people?

Social reasons

BBC GCSE Check and Test: Physical Education

Check the facts

Social reasons

Ability

Most sports require certain physical and mental abilities to perform well.

> **A person's ability can determine both the sport and the level at which it is played.**

Having a high ability in any sport means that there could be increased participation, which in itself can lead to improvement in performance.

Disability

> **Sport for disabled people has changed considerably, with governing bodies devising rules and activities suitable for all disabilities.**

The **Sports Council** published an action plan in 1993 to help disabled people take part in sport.

Seven objectives of the action plan:

- to raise the profile of disabled people in sport
- to ensure that plans for sport include disabled people
- to provide sporting opportunities for disabled people
- to improve access to sport
- to encourage disabled people in international sport
- to ensure the best use of resources and increase finance
- to make sure that the sporting needs of disabled people are met.

Each year, more and more sport is being made available to disabled men and women. Televising wheelchair basketball has helped to raise its profile and media coverage of the **Para-Olympics** has done much to support the cause of disabled people in sport. Most sports centres now make provision for disabled people.

Test yourself

1 List four of the objectives of the Sports Council action plan devised to help disabled people take part in sporting activities.

2 Name two sports in which wheelchair sportsmen and women can compete.

Check the facts

Fewer females take part in sport than males.

> **Each year, 33 % of all men take part in some sporting activity, but only 10 % of women are involved in sport.**

Six reasons why fewer women take part in sport

- **Social attitudes:** it may be difficult for women to commit time to sport if they have 'home' responsibilities.

- **Role models:** for boys, there are many role models in a wide range of sports from athletics, to soccer and rugby; there are fewer role models for girls.

- **Finance:** in most cases, sportswomen do not have as much sponsorship as sportsmen. The top prizes for women in events such as Wimbledon are less then men's prizes.

- **Media coverage:** less media coverage of women in sports means a lower profile, which is linked to sponsorship. There are fewer women involved in the media; newspaper reporters and television presenters are usually men.

- **Coaching:** there are more men than women coaching women's sports teams and individuals.

- **Physique:** see topic 26 for more information on this point.

Social reasons

Test yourself

1 How might social attitudes restrict women's participation in sporting activities?

2 Name two female role models.

3 Explain how aspects of the media may affect females attitudes and participation in sport.

BBC GCSE Check and Test: Physical Education

Check the facts

Family background

These factors can be a major influence on whether or not people participate in sport and leisure activities as children. Some families **support** their children in sport. They may provide money for sports clothes or take them to sporting events. They may take part in sporting and recreational events as a family.

Ethnic background and racism

Ethnic background may also be a factor in the sports people choose to play. There are many Asians playing in first class cricket and on hockey teams, but very few Asians in the English football league. Some football clubs, such as Leicester, have an initiative to encourage more Asians to take part.

Racism is the belief that one race is superior to another. Excluding people from playing or practising a sport or joining a club because of their race or ethnic background is racism. Sadly, there have been instances of spectators verbally abusing players from minority ethnic groups at major sporting events.

Friends

Sometimes, your friends influence how you dress, how you act, and even your participation in sport. This is known as **peer pressure**. Often, friends have similar sporting interests. They may play on the same team at school or in a club. They may enjoy taking part in non-competitive activities, such as mountain biking or casual swimming. However, not all peer pressure is positive, you may be very interested and very good at a sport but your friends may not have that same commitment. Their influence may even force you to give up on some of your sporting activities.

Test yourself

1 What are two ways that families can support their children's participation in sport?

2 What is meant by racism in sport?

3 How might friends affect participation in sporting activities?

Check the facts

Tradition

Tradition can influence participation in sport. Some countries have strong traditions in particular sports, such as cricket in Sri Lanka and the West Indies or ice hockey in Canada. In Wales, rugby union is extremely popular. Sometimes, sports are unique to certain regions of a country, such as wrestling in Cumberland and Westmoreland, rugby league in the north of England or lacrosse in the Manchester area.

Role models

Role models often inspire young people to take up a sport and to strive for the highest levels. The **Sporting Ambassadors Scheme**, where sports stars visit schools, is one way of encouraging participation.

Politics

The government can influence participation by:

- providing funds for facilities
- ensuring time for Physical Education in schools
- promoting sporting activity as beneficial to health.

Test yourself

1 Give examples of sporting activities that might be considered as 'national sports' in certain countries.

2 Why are role models important?

3 What is the Sporting Ambassadors Scheme?

4 How might a national government help with sports participation?

Social reasons

BBC GCSE Check and Test: Physical Education

External influences

Check the facts

The UK Sports Council, now known as UK Sport, was set up in 1997.

It is responsible for **the development of high performance sport** and has four aims:

- to provide the UK's world-class performers with world-class support
- to extend the UK's profile and influence on the international sporting stage
- to promote ethical standards and manage anti-doping programmes
- to create a framework for attracting and running the world's major sporting events

To achieve these aims costs considerable amounts of money; in 2000, the government provided £12.6 million and the National Lottery £20.5 million.

The countries in the UK have their own sports councils:

Sport England

Sport Scotland

The Sports Council for Wales

The Sports Council for Northern Ireland

Sport England's aims are:		
MORE people involved in sport	**MORE** places to play sport	**MORE** medals through higher standards

Sport England has a major role in the distribution of National Lottery money to develop sport. To date, there have been over 7 500 applications for 63 different sports. Over £4 billion has been allocated!

Test yourself

1 What are the four aims of UK Sport?

2 What are the names of the four UK National Sports Councils?

3 What are the aims of Sport England?

Check the facts

Sports governing bodies (National Associations)

There are over 300 national governing bodies in the UK responsible for:

- **Rules** – although, occasionally, changes to rules are made by the international governing body.
- **Competitions** – local, national and international competitions are organised by governing bodies.
- **Team selection** – committees or selectors are responsible for regional and national teams, usually done by having trials.
- **Clubs and players** – resolve disputes between clubs and players, and also discipline clubs and players.
- **Finance** – collect affiliation fees, negotiate deals with media and receive grants from sports councils.
- **Technical advice** – governing bodies are able to give advice to clubs about equipment and facilities.

CCPR stands for **Central Council for Physical Recreation**.

> **The CCPR is a non-governmental body, which is made up of all the national governing bodies.**

The CCPR is split into **six divisions**.

Games and sports	Major spectator sports	Movement and dance	Outdoor pursuits	Water recreation	Interested organisations

The CCPR has **two main objectives**:

- to encourage as many people as possible to participate in all forms of sport and physical recreation.
- to provide the separate governing bodies of the individual sports with a central organisation that represents and promotes their individual and collective interests.

Test yourself

1 Explain four of the responsibilities of governing bodies.

2 What is the purpose of the CCPR?

3 Name three divisions of the CCPR.

External influences

BBC GCSE Check and Test: Physical Education

Check the facts

The BST or **British Sport Trust** is responsible for the administration of:

the Junior Sports Leader Award
the Community Sports Leader Award
the Higher Sports Leader Award
the Basic Expedition Leader Award

> **The YST or Youth Sport Trust was set up in 1994 to improve the sporting provision for all children in the UK.**

Aims of the Youth Sport Trust:

- fun and success in sport
- sports suitable for children's own level
- opportunities to develop a range of sporting skills
- top coaching and resourcing
- development of good sporting attitudes
- positive competition
- a sound foundation for lifelong physical activity.

TOP programmes

1 TOP Tots: simple games, for age 18 months to 3 years.

2 TOP Start: basic movement and skills, for age 3 to 5 years.

3 TOP Play: core skills and fun sports, for age 4 to 9 years.

4 TOP Sport: games skills in football, cricket, netball, hockey, basketball, rounders, rugby, tennis, squash, for age 7 to 11 years.

5 TOP Skill: higher levels and challenge in major games above, for age 11 to 14 years.

6 TOP Link: training for students (age 14 to 19 years) in schools and colleges to run events like TOP Festivals in primary schools.

7 TOP Sportsability: sport opportunities for disabled young people.

8 Millennium volunteers: opportunities to volunteer through sport, for age 16 to 19 years.

Test yourself

1 What are the four awards administered by the BST?

2 Give three aims of the YST.

3 What is the TOP Link programme?

Check the facts

External influences

Entrance fees

Professional sports, such as football, rugby and cricket, hold events that spectators must pay to watch. This fee is often referred to as **gate money** (entrance to football matches is through a turnstile or gate). For special events, such as major cup finals and world championships, the gate money can be considerable!

Semi-professional football clubs often forfeit their right to play at home when drawn against big League opposition. By transferring their game to a club which has a large capacity for spectators, they are guaranteed **more income** than they would get if they played on their own ground.

Merchandising

Spectators often spend money on top of their entrance fee. They might buy **programmes**, **refreshments** and other items such as **flags** and **team strips**. This is referred to as merchandising. The money football and other sports clubs make from merchandising can often exceed the gate money. However, even if it's a world-class event, the revenue spectators bring in may still not be sufficient to cover the players' wages and the staging of the event.

Clubs

Amateur and many semi-professional clubs are supported by their members in a number of ways.

- They may have to pay an annual **subscription** to their club.
- They may pay a **fee** to play and to practice.
- They might have special **fundraising events** such as sponsored activities, jumble sales, raffles and car boot sales.
- Members may **work for their club free of charge** in some way. They may cut the grass at a tennis club, coach a junior section of the club, or offer professional services, such as accountancy (taking care of the clubs finances).

Test yourself

1 What is meant by the term 'gate money', and why might it not be sufficient to meet the cost of a sporting event?

2 Name four items which might be sold in a club shop.

3 How might club members
   a financially support their club?
   b support their club in other ways?

BBC GCSE Check and Test: Physical Education

Check the facts

National government

The national government raises money by taxing individuals and businesses. Money from **taxation** is allocated to government departments. The Minister for Sport in the Department for Culture, Media and Sport then allocates funds to the Sports Councils and local authorities. Taxes are raised in a variety ways: most items purchased have VAT (value added tax); tax is also collected from gambling on sporting events.

Local authorities

Local authorities finance sport through:
- grants from the national government
- council tax
- funds from the Sports Councils
- income from sports facilities such as sports centres
- and the National Lottery.

For more information on local authorities and sport, see topic 78.

National Lottery

The National Lottery started in 1994. For every £1 spent, sport receives 5.6 pence. Although this does not seem like a lot of money, over £17 million is awarded to sport each month through the National Lottery.

National Lottery distribution – where the £1 goes

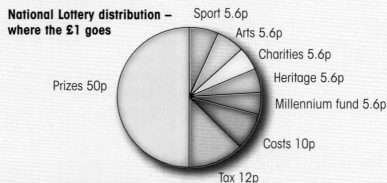

Sport 5.6p
Arts 5.6p
Charities 5.6p
Heritage 5.6p
Millennium fund 5.6p
Costs 10p
Tax 12p
Prizes 50p

Test yourself

1 How does the national government raise money and which department has the decision about where money for sport is to be allocated?

2 How do local authorities raise money?

3 How does the National Lottery benefit sport?

External influences

Check the facts

> **Sponsorship is support for a sport, sport's event, sport's organisation or competitors by an outside body or person for the mutual benefit of both parties.**

Individual sponsorship

World champions, and other top performers, are usually heavily sponsored. **Successful companies want to be associated with successful sportsmen and sportswomen.** Top performers can be sponsored by more than one company. The sponsorship a top football player receives can be more than he is paid by his club! Good, young players, who may be still at school, may receive equipment at a reduced rate, subsidised training facilities or assistance with travel from sponsors.

Team sponsorship

Almost all professional sports clubs have some form of sponsorship, which is identifiable from their badges and logos or even the colour of their team shirts. Premiership football is expensive to sponsor and only very large companies can afford this. Non-league teams, junior teams and school teams often have **local business sponsors**. The cost to these sponsors may only be a set of strips each year, but it will help to promote their name.

National governing bodies

Some sports governing bodies are sponsored and the money provided is often used to help **development**. The Amateur Swimming Association is sponsored by Kiora. This provides extra funding for top competitors and helps to develop the sport with performance badges for beginners.

Competitions

League competitions, prize money, special events and trophies are often sponsored. **The sponsors name then becomes associated with that event**, e.g. the Milk Cup in Schools' Athletics, the Barclays Premiership (Football) or the Stella Artois Tennis Championships.

Test yourself

1 How might a professional sportsman or woman be sponsored?

2 What is the type of sponsorship amateur teams and schools receive?

3 Name two events where the sponsor's name is closely linked.

Check the facts

External influences

The sponsors

Advantages	Disadvantages
• Sponsorship can be powerful advertising.	• Sponsoring unsuccessful events or teams or individuals.
• Popular and televised sponsored events make brand names well known.	• Contractual sponsorship can be for a long period and media coverage may trail off over time.
• Successful individuals and teams make sponsors' names well known.	• The company or product associated with a sport may not be appropriate.
• Certain sponsors become associated with healthy lifestyles and high-level performances.	• The money paid in sponsorship may be very high compared with the amount the company gets back in increased sales.
• Sponsors can pay less tax by giving money to sports.	

Sport and the players

Advantages	Disadvantages
• Rising sports stars are able to train and compete in their sport without having to worry about money and equipment.	• Young players may have their sponsorship withdrawn if their performance does not show improvement.
• It can increase the income of a top athlete.	• Players in less well-known games may not be able to get sponsorship.
• Sport can be promoted by sponsors by the staging of special events.	• Sponsors may want more control over a sport by deciding when and where events are staged.
• Money can improve sport facilities, provide more coaching and encourage participation in a sport.	• Governing bodies of sport may come to rely on sponsorship money.
• New sports can be promoted.	

Test yourself

1 Give two advantages and two disadvantages to a company sponsoring a team.

2 What are the advantages of being sponsored for a professional athelete?

3 How might a sport suffer from being sponsored?

www.bbc.co.uk/revision

Check the facts

We are surrounded by sports' pictures, broadcasts and adverts. Sports' coverage is now a multi-million pound business.

Newspapers

Newspapers often have a lot of information about sport, e.g. in depth coverage of events, analysis of results, league tables, etc.. All newspapers have **sports sections**, some even have **pull-out supplements**. However, in order to sell papers, stories of events and personalities are often sensationalised. In addition, although there may be in depth coverage, it is usually one day old when it is reported.

Magazines

Sports magazines contain information about personalities and forthcoming events. There may be game plans and/or performance statistics. They are often **a good reference for particular sports**. However, they do not often cover current news about events, particularly if they are only published monthly.

CD-ROMs

CD-ROMs, which **store large amounts of information**, may contain text, video clips and sound. The many encyclopaedias on CD-ROM often include information about sports, sporting events and sports personalities.

Radio

Radio commentators are skilled at describing events, setting the scene and giving facts and figures. Although live commentary provides **up-to-the-minute detail of events**, it may not be appropriate for many sporting events. Whilst it is possible to follow the action in a rugby match, it is difficult to broadcast gymnastics or archery. Local radio plays an important part in many communities, giving information and match commentary on local teams.

Test yourself

1 Give one advantage and one disadvantage of a match report appearing in a newspaper.

2 Apart from match reports, what other sport-related articles appear in newspapers?

3 Suggest two sports which the listener could easily follow on the radio and two which would be more difficult.

External influences

BBC GCSE Check and Test: Physical Education

Check the facts

Television

All major sporting events are shown on television.

Some events, such as one-day cricket, were invented for television. Television stations bid against each other for the right to screen most popular events. The advent of satellite television in 1992 brought further opportunities to broadcast sport, with three dedicated sports channels, as well as a variety of other sporting channels such as Eurosport and Extreme sports. No doubt digital television channels will also have a big impact on sport. Already, the collapse of ITV Digital in 2002 has left some football clubs bankrupt.

Positives	Negatives
• minority sports popularised, e.g. American football	• effect on individuals and teams, e.g. can give bad publicity
• new events, e.g. indoor windsurfing	• rules and timing of events, e.g. events arranged to suit best viewing times and not competitors
• new technology, e.g. miniature cameras on cricket stumps	• television equipment, e.g. bright lights, intrusive cameras
• refereeing, e.g. video replay in rugby	• contradiction of decisions, e.g. replays after events
• sports development, e.g. money paid to governing bodies	• excessive coverage, e.g. reduced interest in sports
• promoting sport, e.g. participation and healthy lifestyles	• media influence, e.g. promote some sports and ignore others
• access, e.g. worldwide events	
• better coverage, e.g. golf easier to follow on TV	

Test yourself

1 Video replay in rugby helps referees to decide whether or not a try has been scored. Select two games of your choice and suggest how video evidence might benefit each game.

2 How does television coverage affect when some events take place?

3 What sporting events are best watched on television (instead of being a spectator in the crowd)? Give two examples.

Check the facts

Local authorities are local government administrative bodies, such as town, city, district or county councils.

These authorities control two important areas: education and leisure departments; which **provide sporting and recreational facilities**.

Education departments

Schools and community colleges, which come under the control of education departments, are **required to provide facilities for physical education**. These may range from basic gyms and grass playing-fields to swimming pools, sports halls and floodlit pitches. Schools may hire their facilities to clubs after normal school hours. This is known as dual use. Sometimes facilities are used by both the school and the local community. This is known as joint provision.

Leisure departments

These control and maintain a wide range of sport and leisure **facilities more accessible to the public** than schools and colleges. These include leisure centres, sports halls, playing-fields, athletic tracks, golf courses, bowling greens, swimming pools and tennis courts.

The running costs of sports facilities are often high, particularly swimming pools. Local authorities will subsidise these as it is unlikely that the income from swimmers will meet the necessary costs such as heating, lighting, reception and lifeguards.

Test yourself

1 What is the difference between dual use and joint provision?

2 How might joint provision benefit a school or college?

3 What is the role of a leisure department in a local authority?

4 What is meant by a subsidy?

5 The running costs of swimming pools are high. What local authority sports facilities might have very low running costs?

Organisation and provision

BBC GCSE Check and Test: Physical Education

Check the facts

Hotels

Many hotels now have **leisure suites for guests and non-residents**. These usually consist of a fitness room, with resistance machines, free weights and a swimming pool. Larger rural hotels may have small golf courses and tennis courts. Guests usually have free use of these facilities whilst local residents can take out membership of the hotel 'leisure club'.

Some **holiday complexes** are now based around central leisure facilities with large swimming pools and a range of outdoor activity areas.

Commercial sports clubs

Commercial clubs may often provide a local facility that is **not subsidised by the local authority**. The most popular private clubs are golf clubs, however, squash and tennis clubs are also well used. Fitness and leisure clubs, which are not attached to hotels, also increase local provision.

Voluntary organisations

Voluntary organisations, such as local badminton clubs or cricket clubs, provide opportunities for members to participate in sport. They mainly own their own facilities, perhaps tennis courts or cricket grounds, but are **not commercial organisations intent on making a profit**. Most are long established. Very few newly formed clubs are able to purchase their own facilities and must rent from their local authority instead.

Company sports clubs

Larger companies sometimes have sports and social clubs that are **subsidised by the company**. Facilities usually include playing-fields, changing rooms, team strips and help with travel.

 Test yourself

1 How do hotels contribute to the provision of local leisure facilities?

2 What is the difference between a commercial sports club and a voluntary sports club?

3 How might a large company support leisure activities for its work force?

Check the facts

The functions of a sports club

- To provide facilities and opportunities for its members to play the sport and meet socially.
- To organise competitions and matches.
- To encourage people to take part in their sport.
- To develop policies that encourage junior members, so that there is continual growth in the club.
- To become involved in the local community.

Members

People who belong to a club are its members. The members take part in the club's activities, although in some clubs members may not be very active.

Committees

Club members usually elect a smaller number of people to look after the club's affairs. This is usually known as a committee, and these are the **officials** of the club. (Not to be confused with match officials who control the games.) In most clubs, the officials are voluntary, in larger clubs, they may be paid.

The **chairperson** is the most important official in the club. He or she controls committee meetings and represents the club at special events. If the chairperson is ill or unable to attend a meeting then the **vice-chairperson** will stand in.

Secretaries arrange committee meetings and reply to letters. During a meeting they will take notes; these are known as minutes. The **treasurer** is responsible for the club's finances, for collecting subscriptions from members and for paying club bills.

In larger clubs, there may be other officials such as a fixtures secretary, a member responsible for team selection, a coach, a trainer or a physiotherapist. There might be a president, vice-president or a patron. They are not usually involved with the running of a club, but are appointed to these positions because they might raise the profile of the club and improve its image. Patrons may also make financial donations to the club.

Test yourself

1 Name three functions of a sports club.

2 Name three club officials.

3 What is the role of a club president or patron?

Organisation and provision

BBC GCSE Check and Test: Physical Education

Organisation and provision

Check the facts

For most sportsmen and women, international sport is their ambition.

> **Top sportsmen and women bring recognition of their country to the rest of the world.**

Governments are well aware of how successful teams and individuals raise the image of their country.

International competitions

Competition between **teams or individuals from different countries** has a long history. An England cricket team played against America in 1844. There was an England v Scotland footbal match in 1870 and an England v Scotland rugby union match in 1871.

Continental championships

The world is divided into **continents**: Asia, North America, South America, Australasia, Africa, Antartica and Europe. Continental championships include the Europa Cup (athletics), the Cup of Nations (African football championships), the Asian Swimming Championships and the Pan American Athletics Championships.

World championships

World championships in some sports are relatively new. Rugby union's first world championship was 100 years after the first international match. In tennis and golf, there are no world championships, but there are **Grand Slam** events. The rankings of the top players are worked out by computer on their results throughout the season.

Olympic games

The goal of the Olympic Movement is to contribute to **building a peaceful and better world by educating youth through sport** practised without discrimination of any kind and in the Olympic spirit, which requires mutual understanding with a spirit of friendship, solidarity and fair play. The Olympic motto is *Citius, Altius, Fortius,* which is Latin for Fastest, Highest, Strongest.

Test yourself

1 What is an international competition?

2 Give two examples of continental competitions.

3 What is the Olympic motto in English?

www.bbc.co.uk/revision

Check the facts

When a city or country hosts an international event, the host's competitors will have some advantage. **Crowd support**, **less travel** and **positive media coverage** are all important factors.

> **The costs and potential rewards of staging international events are considerable.**

However, **as events get bigger**, with more sports and more competitors, **organisation becomes more difficult**. Even staging international rugby, cricket or football matches can be costly and need to be planned well in advance.

Questions which organisers need to ask are:

- Are the facilities good enough for the competition?
- Where will all the competitors stay?
- Will spectators get to see the competitions?
- Who will provide funding for the competition?
- What security arrangements need to be made?
- What television coverage will there be?

Advantages	Disadvantages
• More and better sports facilities are built.	• The increased number of people can cause a major disruption to the everyday life of the residents.
• Access, transport and hotels are improved.	• Finance needed to build new/improve old facilities might be diverted from areas such as education or healthcare.
• Increased tourism and business.	
• More work in building facilities and staffing the events.	
• The city or country will become well known.	• Security to control crowds and prevent terrorists is expensive.
• The nation might become more united.	• Extra staff may be unfamiliar with the city.

Test yourself

1 What are two of the main concerns organisers might have in staging a major international event such as the Commonwealth Games?

2 Give two advantages the staging of a major sporting event, such as the World Student Games, may bring to a city.

3 Why might financing a major sporting event be a disadvantage for a town or city, or even a country?

Organisation and provision

BBC GCSE Check and Test: Physical Education

Check the facts

'The most important thing in the Olympic Games is not to win, but to take part. Just as the most important thing in life is not the triumph, but the struggle. The essential thing is not to have conquered but to have fought well.'

Baron Pierre de Coubertin, founder of the modern Olympic Games

Summer Games fact file

Finance: the cost of the first modern games in **Athens** (1896) was higher than expected. The stadium in **Montreal** (1976) was unfinished at the start of the Games. In **Los Angeles** (1984), major sponsorship and marketing deals were necessary to meet the costs. There was even more sponsorship, particularly from Coca Cola, for the **Atlanta** Games (1998). Although costs rose to an estimated $2.4 billion (AUD), television rights and sponsorship managed to cover them all in **Sydney** (2000).

Politics: controversy broke out over the display of national flags at the **London** Games (1908). Germany was banned from competing in **Antwerp** (1920) and in **Paris** (1924) because of its involvement in WW1. When the Games were held in **Berlin** (1936), they provided a showcase for Hitler and Nazi propaganda. In **Melbourne** (1956), a number of teams withdrew for political reasons for the first time. This happened again in **Moscow** (1980) when the Americans withdrew and in **Los Angeles** (1984) when the USSR withdrew. Trouble between Israelis and Palestinians ended with hostages, officials and terrorists being killed at the **Munich** Games (1972).

Competitors: Black athlete, Jesse Owens, won four gold medals in **Berlin** (1936), but Hitler refused to present them. Other outstanding performances include Dick Fosbury in **Mexico** (1968) with his unique high jump style, and Steven Redgrave collecting his fifth gold medal in **Sydney** (2000).

Cheating: Fred Lorz, the marathon 'winner' in **St Louis** (1904), went part way by car. Jim Thorpe, the decathlon winner in **Stockholm** (1912), was actually a professional. In many Games, there have been a minority taking drugs, but the most famous example was Ben Johnson in **Seoul** (1988).

Test yourself

1 To stage the Olympics is extremely expensive for a country. In what way did Australia and the USA fund the Games?

2 Select and explain one 'political' event that has occurred at the Games.

3 Choose one Olympic competitor and explain why he or she has been important for their sport.

www.bbc.co.uk/revision

Check the facts

> Launched in 2000, the UK Sports Institute is made up of the English Institute of Sport, the Scottish Institute of Sport, the Welsh Insitute of Sport and the Sports Institute Northern Ireland.

Objectives

- Expert advice
- Personal development and training
- Coaching
- Support staff
- Specialist facilities
- Resources
- Scientific and medical services

The Institute is based on these existing National Sports Centres.

Location	Specialist activities
Crystal Palace, England	swimming, badminton, **athletics**
Holme Pierpoint/Loughborough University, England	rowing, **sailing**, canoeing, water sports
Bisham Abbey, England	**tennis**, weightlifting, rugby, hockey
Lilleshall, England	**soccer**, gymnastics, squash, volleyball, golf
Plas y Brenin, Wales	outdoor activities, **mountaineering**
Cumbrae, Scotland	**water sports** and related activities
Inverclyde, Scotland	gymnastics, squash, golf, **hockey**
Aviemore, Scotland	**skiing** and other outdoor activities
Cardiff, Wales	basket ball, **gymnastics**, badminton, swimming, tennis
Caenarfon, Wales	**water sports**
Tollymore, N. Ireland	**outdoor activities**

The ten centres of excellence for sport are:

Bath University   Bedford   Bisham Abbey   Crystal Palace   Gateshead

Holme Pierpoint/Loughborough University   Lilleshall   Manchester

Southampton University   Sheffield

Test yourself

1 Name four objectives of the UK Sports Institute.

2 What are the main sporting activities held at:
   (a) Holme Pierpoint? **(b)** Plas y Brenin? **(c)** Aviemore? **(d)** Tollymore?

3 Name three centres of excellence which are not based at the National Sports Centres.

Check the facts

Organisation and provision

> **The majority of people who play sport at the present time are amateurs.**

They play for **fun** and **enjoyment**. However, in every sport there are a group of professionals who earn their living from their sport. It may be playing, coaching or in the administration of events. Since the relaxation of rules, particularly in rugby union, there are many more semi-professionals.

At one time, there was little opportunity for amateurs to compete either against or on the same team as professionals; although, sports such as golf, cricket, tennis and badminton have been **open** for some time.

Becoming a professional

Advantages	Disadvantages
• They can earn a lot of money. • Professional sportspersons become popular. • They can perfect their game. • They are wanted by the media for interviews. • They travel the world to compete at the highest level. • They are paid to do something they enjoy. • They can retire early.	• Injury can ruin a career. • At the highest level, there is a lot of travel. • There are always new young competitors challenging for a top place. • It can be very stressful for an individual to keep his or her place at the top. • The ability to maintain fitness and performance usually decreases with age. • Once their career is over, they may have little training to do another job.

Test yourself

1 What is meant by open competitions?

2 What are two benefits of becoming a professional sportsperson?

3 Why might a professional sportsperson become less successful as they get older?

Check the facts

> Before taking part in a sporting activity, it is important that the activity area is checked for any hazards.

Gymnasia and sports halls

- floor surfaces clear of debris
- quality of mats
- security and safe storage of equipment
- clearance around sides of courts
- safety of football goals

Swimming pools

- emergency telephone
- availability of rescue aids
- marked diving area
- security and storage of equipment on poolside
- emergency procedure

Playing fields, including artificial surfaces

- playing surfaces clear of debris
- posts secure
- even playing surface

Athletics

- track surfaces even and clear of debris
- jumping pits clear of debris
- safe landing areas for high jump and pole vault
- safe areas for throwing events

Outdoor and adventurous activities

- consideration and preparation for weather conditions
- emergency procedure
- specific activity risk, e.g. climbing grade

Test yourself

1 What problems might you find with the floor surfaces in a gymnasium or sports hall?

2 What is the most likely dangerous hazard on the playing surface of an outdoor pitch?

3 Why might a swimming pool be considered a high risk area?

4 Why is it important that weather conditions are taken into account before a mountain walk?

Health and safety

BBC GCSE Check and Test: Physical Education

Check the facts

Health and safety

> **Some sporting activities are very high risk and others are very low risk.**

- **Throwing events** in athletics are hazardous for the competitors, judges and spectators; but, in green bowls, there are fewer risks!

- There are higher risks in **invasion games** where body contact, as in rugby, is part of the game.

- In **striking games**, there are risks in being struck by the ball (and, occasionally, the bat).

- **Swimming** is a particular hazard for weak or inexperienced swimmers in swimming pools, and the risk increases considerably when the water is cold and moving as in a sea or river.

- **Gymnastics** and trampolining can be high risk activities even for high-level performers when they are learning new skills.

- **Outdoor activities** such as a walk in the hills in good summer weather has considerably less risk than the same walk in poor winter weather.

Test yourself

1 Put the following activities in order from high to low risk.
(a) for competitors   **(b)** for spectators
sailing swimming hammer-throwing rugby trampolining

2 Why might invasion games be considered higher risk than net games? Use examples to illustrate your answer.

3 How might swimming become an even higher risk for weak or inexperienced swimmers?

4 In what circumstances might an experienced gymnast perform a high risk activity?

Check the facts

Physical and mental preparation and recovery

Warming up and cooling down is an essential part of any physical activity. Playing at the **correct level** for age or ability can prevent injury. In sports such as boxing and judo, levels are associated with age and weight, which ensure that contests are fair. Taking part within your capabilities is particularly important in outdoor activities, for instance, attempting climbs at the right level or canoeing, sailing or surfing in conditions in which you can cope.

Playing by the rules

Rules are designed to enable play to take place and to reduce the injury risk to competitors and spectators. Waiting for an umpire before bowling in cricket and rounders ensures the batsmen and women are ready. In athletics, it is important to **wait for a signal** to jump or throw for the safety of officials and other competitors. **Correct tackling** in hockey, football and rugby ensures the safety of the person being tackled and even the person making the tackle.

Correct equipment

Most activities with a high risk of injury require the competitors to wear the correct equipment. Safety **helmets** are essential when practising and playing with hard cricket balls. In football, players are required to wear **shin pads** and there are regulations about the length of studs on boots. The wearing of jewellery can be a danger to oneself and others. Even tying back long hair is important. **Mouthguards** are now common at most levels of rugby. In outdoor activities, it is essential to have the correct equipment, not just footwear and **waterproofs** for hill walking and lifejackets for water sports, but also safety and **survival equipment**. Equipment must also be checked regularly for safety; items such as ski-bindings, cycles, climbing equipment and similar items, which can become worn and ineffective.

Test yourself

1 Explain why warming up and cooling down is important in any sporting activity.

2 Give examples of two rules, from sports of your choice, that safeguard competitors from injury.

3 Name two items of equipment that might prevent injury to a player.

Health and safety

BBC GCSE Check and Test: Physical Education

Health and safety

Check the facts

- **Accidents:** most injuries are caused through accidents. In athletics, a runner can easily be tripped in the crowded start of a long distance race. Slipping because of poor footwear in football or being hit with a hockey ball are other accidents. Sometimes, a player may damage themselves by moving or twisting too quickly.

- **Contact sports:** in combat sports, such as boxing and wrestling, contact is the essential element. In rugby, contact is an integral part of the game during scrummaging and tackling. In football, fair contact can be made by players challenging for the ball. In some invasion games, such as basketball and hockey, there is no contact (officially), but it often occurs.

- **Foul play:** players can be injured in games when the rules are broken. Many rules are devised to keep players safe from injury, as well as providing a pattern to the game. In rugby, tackling around the neck and, in hockey, lifting the ball near a player, can cause injury to other players and are against the rules of these games.

- **Overuse:** repeating actions in sports can cause damage to muscles, tendons, ligaments and bone. High-level performers need to practice individual skills over and over again and then repeat them in a match situation. A cricketer may spend many hours in bowling practice. He may play most days of the week, and have to bowl thousands of balls during a season. Professional players may even have to play when injured causing further damage to their bodies.

- **Equipment:** incorrect or ill-fitting equipment may cause injury. Marathon runners need to run considerable distances most days and, therefore, running shoes must be suitable for running on hard surfaces and fit well. Bindings on skis must be at the right tension to keep the ski attached to the boot, but release it on impact to prevent damage to the skier's legs. Equipment may break during use; in pole vaulting this can be extremely dangerous!

Test yourself

1 Name two sports where physical contact is part of the game.

2 Give three examples of equipment failure causing injury to a performer.

Check the facts

The body

> **Keeping the skin clean is not only an important way of resisting infection, but also of preventing body odour.**

During sporting activity, the body sweats and in many activities, such as hockey and rugby, dirt from the fields covers the body and clothing. **Showering and washing with soap and water is a simple and effective way of cleaning the body.**

Feet must be kept healthy; correctly fitting footwear for sport and activity is essential. Corns, bunions and blisters are caused by poor quality and ill-fitting shoes.

Two common infections of the feet

- **Athletes foot:** a fungal growth between the toes. Usually occurring next to the little toes, this fungal growth develops in warm moist places. The skin cracks, peels and becomes itchy. It is easily spread to other people by contact from floors and shared towels.
- **Verrucas:** these are warts on the feet. They spread easily through a virus, are difficult to get rid of and are often painful.

Keeping feet clean and drying them well helps minimise the chance of infection. If either of these infections are contracted, **proper foot hygiene** becomes even more important and treatment is necessary.

Clothing and equipment

Clothing should be washed regularly as it absorbs body sweat and bacteria from the skin. Underclothes and socks are of particular importance. A complete change of clothing for sport is best and materials such as cotton are preferable to nylon. In outdoor activities, breathable waterproof clothing is essential for comfort. Walking and climbing boots need to be cleaned and waterproofed. Sports shoes should be regularly cleaned, particularly the insoles. Football and rugby boots should be cleaned and studs checked for wear to prevent injury to oneself and others. Equipment also needs to be cleaned and maintained.

Test yourself

1 Give two reasons for showering after sporting activities.

2 What are two common foot infections and how can they be prevented?

3 Why is it important to wash sports clothes after use?

Health and safety

BBC GCSE Check and Test: Physical Education

Types of injury and treatment

Check the facts

There are many types of sporting injury that can be treated quickly and effectively on the spot.

A common treatment for many soft tissue injuries is the RICE method.

R **Rest** is necessary because continued use of the damaged muscle will cause even more damage and make the recovery time longer.

I **Ice** applied to the injury will reduce swelling and pain.

C **Compressing** the area will provide support.

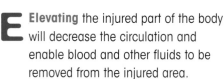

E **Elevating** the injured part of the body will decrease the circulation and enable blood and other fluids to be removed from the injured area.

Test yourself

1 Explain what is meant by the RICE method of treatment, giving details of each part of the process.

www.bbc.co.uk/revision

Check the facts

- **Skin injuries:** usually as the result of a sliding fall on a rough surface, layers of skin are scraped off. This is known as an **abrasion**. It may be painful, but it is not serious.

  Treatment: wounds need to be **cleaned and dressed**. Larger and deeper cuts may need to be **stitched**. If blood is strongly pumping out of a cut, then it is important to stop blood flow and get **medical help**. To stop serious bleeding, a clean pad needs to be applied and firmly held in place.

- **Blisters:** repeated actions that involve **friction** can cause blisters. These occur on the feet because of ill-fitting shoes, but they can also occur on the hands in racket games and gymnastics.

  Treatment: small blisters can be left or covered with tape. Larger blisters may have to be **punctured** to release fluid and enable the skin to rebuild.

- **Muscle bruising:** this is a common injury in contact sports, such as rugby and soccer. A **hard impact** on the surface of the muscle results in a bruise. The blood vessels just below the skin, and deeper depending on the strength of impact, are ruptured (burst).

  Treatment: **ice** applied to the bruise reduces the swelling and blood flow and reduces the pain.

- **Muscle tears and pulls:** athletes can often damage muscles internally by **applying too much force** in moving their own bodies or an external object. Insufficient warm up can lead to this type of injury.

  Treatment: **RICE** treatment is most effective. Damaged muscle repairs itself and, depending on the extent of the damage, it could be working near full strength within seven days.

- **Muscle cramp:** a muscle or group of muscles go into **involuntary spasm**. Cramp can occur during swimming when the muscles are chilled or due to a lack of salt and minerals. **Stitch** is cramp in the diaphragm.

  Treatment: as the muscles are in a state of tension, they need to be mechanically **stretched**. Cramp can often occur in the calf muscle, which can be stretched by pulling the foot towards the knee. Push a **clenched fist** into the diaphragm area to relieve the symptoms of stitch.

Test yourself

1 How do blisters occur and what is their treatment?

2 What is the most common muscle injury in contact sports?

3 What is the most frequent cause of muscle tears and what is suitable treatment?

Types of injury and treatment

BBC GCSE Check and Test: Physical Education

Types of injury and treatment

Check the facts

Ligaments

> **The ligaments hold joints together.**

Excessive force on a joint can result in a **sprain** or, more seriously, a **rupture.** A common injury for football players is to the cruciate ligaments in the knee. Sudden turning during the game can cause these ligaments to be damaged. In some cases, artificial ligaments are fitted inside the knee allowing people to continue to participate in their sport.

Treatment: RICE treatment can be used for a minor sprain, but in more serious cases, **medical treatment** will be needed.

Tendons

> **Tendons attach muscle to a bone.**

Strong movements, particularly jumping, apply very high forces to tendons. Tendons can be **partially torn** or **ruptured.** The **Achilles tendon** can often be damaged in badminton and squash.

Treatment: RICE can be used in less severe cases with considerable rest. Where a rupture of the tendon occurs, then **surgery** is required to join the tendon together again.

Tendonitis

Tendons can become **inflamed** with constant use causing tendonitis. The most common is tennis elbow as a result of repeated arm movements. Golfers experience tendonitis in a different part of the elbow.

Treatment: **physiotherapy** and stretching exercises can help relieve pain and encourage healing. In extreme cases, **cortisone injections** may be necessary if tendonitis becomes chronic.

Test yourself

1 What is a sprain and how can it be treated?

2 What is the most common knee injury for football players?

3 What is a common injury for badminton and squash players?

4 What is tendonitis and why does it occur?

> If there is pressure to move the joint in the wrong direction, the internal structure of the joint can be damaged.

Cartilage can be torn with excessive and incorrect movement. In football, many players suffer damage to the cartilage in the knee because of the twisting and turning of the leg during the game.

Treatment: in severe cases, cartilage may be badly torn causing the knee joint to be locked. **Medical help** will be needed. In less severe cases, the sportsperson may be able to walk but, ultimately, **surgery** will be required.

Dislocation

A dislocated joint

Extreme pressure on the joint can cause the joint to **break apart**. One bone is moved from its normal position in the joint. In a ball and socket joint, the ball comes out of the socket. When this occurs, there is often **damage to the surrounding tissues, ligaments and tendons**. Dislocation of the shoulder joint can occur in rugby where there is often considerable impact on the shoulder during tackling.

Humerus

Radius

Ulna

Treatment: medical treatment is needed for this injury. Joints are often **relocated** under anaesthetic at a hospital. Because the ligaments and tendons are stretched during a dislocation, the joint can become much weaker and be prone to dislocation. **Surgery** may be needed to prevent this from happening in the future.

1 What is the main cause of knee joint injury in football?

2 What is meant by dislocation of a joint? Give an example from a sport of how a dislocation might occur.

3 When a joint is dislocated, what further damage might occur to the joint?

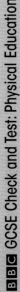

Types of injury and treatment

BBC GCSE Check and Test: Physical Education

Types of injury and treatment

Check the facts

> **Bones can be broken because they are rigid.**

Direct blows and **awkward falls** can result in broken bones. Some breaks, such as toes and fingers, may be inconvenient rather than serious, but breaks to the larger bones of the arms, legs and vertebrae are more serious.

Three types of fracture

- **Simple fractures:** the bone is broken cleanly and does not pierce the skin.

- **Compound fractures:** parts of the broken bone come through the surface of the skin.

- **Greenstick fractures:** this often occurs in young children where the bones are soft and do not break cleanly, but splinter instead.

Treatment: if a fracture is suspected, then the person needs to be kept warm and comfortable until medical help arrives. **Bones heal themselves over time**. However, most bones need to be **set properly** first and a **plaster cast or splint** fixed to the injured area in order to immobilise it.

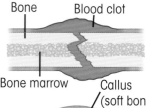

After a bone injury, blood oozes out of broken blood vessels, and forms a clot around the jagged edge of bone.

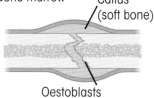

Connective tissue forms a callus (soft bone) to hold broken ends together. Oestoblasts (special cells) strengthen the bone ends.

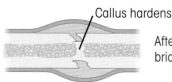

After some time, the callus hardens, bridging the gap between bone ends.

Bone healing

www.bbc.co.uk/revision

Test yourself

1 What is the difference between simple and greenstick fractures?

2 In what circumstances does a greenstick fracture occur?

3 Explain the three stages of bone healing using simple diagrams.

Check the facts

Hyperventilation

After **heavy exercise** or when a person is **very anxious**, hyperventilation can occur. Breathing speeds up, resulting in the lungs **exhaling large amounts of carbon dioxide** (CO_2).

Treatment: to reduce the breathing rate, the person must be **calmed down**. **Breathing into a paper bag** restores the breathing rate to a normal level.

Shock

Being involved in an accident, even if not injured, can bring about shock in a person. He or she may look **pale**, have a **rapid pulse**, **breathe shallowly** or even **yawn** or **feel faint**.

Treatment: **treat the cause of the shock**, if possible. Keep the person warm and lying down with his or her head low. Check the person's breathing and pulse and send for **medical help**.

Hypothermia

The **body temperature falls below 35°** Celcius. Although this usually occurs during outdoor activities, people can suffer from hypothermia even on the playing field if the weather is very cold.

Treatment: the person should be **moved out of the adverse conditions** and insulated with **extra clothing**, including his or her head. If the person is conscious, give him or her **hot drinks**.

Hyperthermia

The **body temperature rises above 39°** Celcius. Excessive physical exercise in hot and sunny conditions can cause hyperthermia. The body is **unable to get rid of sufficient heat** through sweating. Too much sweating leads to **dehydration**.

Treatment: the person should be **moved to a cool and breezy place**. Dehydration needs to be treated with **water** to restore body fluids. In the case of heat exhaustion, give the person a weak **solution of salt and water**.

Test yourself

1 What is the best way to deal with hyperventilation?

2 Why might shock occur?

3 Explain the difference between hypothermia and hyperthermia and how these conditions occur.

Types of injury and treatment

BBC GCSE Check and Test: Physical Education

Check the facts

**Asthma is a respiratory problem
leading to breathing fits.**

Many sportsmen and women are able to take a full and active part in
sporting events, even though they suffer from asthma. Most are able to
control the onset and effects of asthma with a wide range of drugs.

Asthma attack

This can be brought on by adverse weather conditions, exercise or lack of
control drugs. Breathing becomes difficult – there is **a shortness of breath
and wheezing**.

Treatment: the **activity needs to be stopped** and, where possible, an
inhaler used. In severe cases, the person should be put in the recovery
position and someone should get medical help.

Test yourself

1 What must asthma sufferers take regularly?

2 What might bring on an asthma attack?

3 What should be done immediately at the onset of an asthma attack?

4 What should be done in the case of a severe attack?

Check the facts

In emergencies where medical help is not immediately available, being able to give treatment may well save the person's life.

Although it is always best to get medical help immediately when an injury is serious, this is not always possible. The injured person may be on a sports field, in a forest or on a mountain and it may be hours before qualified medical help can get there.

A common treatment for emergencies is the DRABC routine.

D **Danger.** Ensure that you are not in danger and that the casualty is no longer in danger.

R **Response.** Check whether or not the casualty can respond to you and, if so, ask for information about his or her injuries.

A **Airways.** Are they clear so that the casualty can breathe? Remove any debris with your finger.

B **Breathing.** Is the casualty breathing? Check the chest is moving and listen for breathing.

C **Circulation.** Check the casualty's pulse to confirm circulation.

Types of injury and treatment

Test yourself

1 In the DRABC routine, what is the first thing you must do?

2 Why would you want the casualty to respond to you?

3 How might the casualty's airways be blocked and what procedure would you use to clear airways?

4 How can you check circulation?

BBC GCSE Check and Test: Physical Education

Types of injury and treatment

Check the facts

Mouth-to-mouth resuscitation

Once breathing stops, **the brain is starved of oxygen**, therefore, it is essential that every attempt should be made to restart the breathing as quickly as possible. Mouth-to-mouth resuscitation is when **air is blown into the casualty's lungs**. While the person is being resuscitated, someone should **urgently get medical help** through the emergency services.

Procedure

1 Check that the airways are clear. If there is debris lodged in the back of the throat, it must be pulled out. The head should be tilted back so that the airway through the trachea to the lungs is clear.
2 The person's nose needs to be nipped. Then, take a large breath which has to be forced into the person's lungs from mouth to mouth. This should make the person's chest rise as the lungs are filled with air.
3 Take your mouth away. The person will exhale due to the lungs contracting.
4 The action should be repeated at the rate of one breath every six seconds. This should be continued until the person breathes normally, or medical help arrives.
5 Check the pulse at the end of each minute.

Cardiac massage

If there is no pulse, then the heart has stopped beating. This is known as **cardiac arrest** and the heart needs to be restarted. Cardiac massage is one method of doing this. **External pressure is applied to the chest above the heart**. It is also important to send for medical help immediately.

Procedure

1 The person is laid on his or her back. The point to apply pressure is found one inch above the lowest rib where it joins the sternum (breast bone).
2 The heel of the hand is pressed at this point with the other hand on top.
3 By leaning over, weight can be applied to depress the sternum by about 4–5 cms.
4 Pressure should be applied at the rate of 80 times per minute.
5 The pulse needs to be checked every minute. When it returns, massage can be stopped.

Test yourself

1 Explain the procedure for mouth-to-mouth resuscitation.
2 Explain the procedure for cardiac massage.

Check the facts

Performer: a **person taking part** in a sporting activity.

Teacher: the main role of a teacher is to introduce children and students to sporting activities through **physical education lessons**. The teacher will usually have particular skills and knowledge in some sports and will use these to help pupils to reach even higher levels through **school clubs** and teams in **extra-curricular activities**.

School sports coordinator: first appointed in 2000, a school sports coordinator's key tasks are to establish and **develop PE and sport in primary schools**; **establish links between schools and local sports clubs**; establish and **support after school and inter-school sports**; and **develop leadership and coaching programmes** for senior students.

Coach: a coach is usually a **specialist in one sporting activity**. He or she may have been a player before becoming a coach. Coaches are supported by the National Coaching Foundation, who provide training.

Trainer: larger sports clubs may have a trainer who takes responsibility for the **physical preparation** of players. He or she will have a good knowledge of the game and an understanding of types of fitness required and training methods.

Official: sports events need officials to **take charge of the game**. In recreational games, there are usually no officials and the players themselves take charge of the game. However, in organised competitions, officials are necessary. The complexity of the game and the level of competition often determines the number of officials. A club tennis tournament match might only have an umpire, but for a Wimbledon match, there are many more officials, each with highly specialised jobs and an umpire having overall control. Officials must have a **very good knowledge of the rules**, particularly when they are complicated, as in golf. The use of video replays to help officials is now becoming common and is extensively used in both rugby and cricket. In athletics, swimming and cycling, photo-finish cameras assist officials with decision-making.

Test yourself

1 Name two of the tasks of a school sports coordinator.

2 What is the difference between a coach and a trainer?

3 How might a person become a coach?

4 When might a sporting activity require few, if any, officials?

Practical activities

BBC GCSE Check and Test: Physical Education

Answers

01 Function
1 Protection, support, movement and blood production
2 The brain and spinal cord, protected by the cranium and the vertebral column
3 Red and white blood cells

02 Bones
1 They are strong and their bone marrow produces red and white blood cells.
2 In the wrist and ankles
3 They form large surface areas for the skull and provide good protection.

03 Types of joints
1 The skull and pelvis
2 The ribs to the sternum – there is no joint cavity; bones are connected by cartilage.
3 They contain synovial fluid.

04 Synovial joints
1 A capsule filled with synovial fluid.
2 Elbow or knee joint, one plane of movement – throwing a ball, kicking a football
3 The pivot joint is in the neck and allows movement of the head.

05 Cartilage and ligaments
1 Articular cartilage – reduces friction; fibro cartilage – a shock absorber
2 Ligaments are strong connective tissue that hold joints together.

06 Types of body movement
1 Running
2 Rotation
3 Adduction

07 Muscle types and structures
1 Smooth, cardiac and voluntary
2 Muscle fibres shorten
3 Slow twitch in swimming, cycling and running when at a steady pace; but fast twitch in sprints at finish

08 Muscle action
1 Partial contraction of muscles
2 Triceps; muscles in the shoulders and back such as the trapezius
3 Tendons attach muscles to bones, at the origin and insertion.

09 Muscle contraction
1 Isometric, isokinetic, isotonic
2 Pushing in a scrum
3 When lifting a bar in a bicep curl, the bicep muscle shortens.

10 Levers
1 Load is the weight of the body; fulcrum is the ball of the foot.
2 Diagram should identify force, load and fulcrum of quadriceps machine.
3 Bicep curl is a third order lever with the fulcrum at the elbow.

11 Blood vessels and circulation
1 Transports blood, maintains body temperature, protection by taking white blood cells to areas of infection
2 Arteries carry oxygenated blood away from the heart. The pulmonary artery carries deoxygenated blood from heart to lungs.
3 Veins carry blood back to the heart under low pressure. Valves stop blood from flowing in the wrong direction.

12 The heart
1 The aorta is the main artery from the heart to the rest of the body.
2 The bicuspid valve stops blood going back.
3

right atrium	left atrium
right ventricle	left ventricle

13 Blood
1 Red blood cells carry oxygen.
2 a Red blood cells
  b Plasma
3 It carries white blood cells to the site of infection.

14 Effects of exercise
1 Carotid in the neck, radial in the wrist
2 The volume of blood leaving the ventricle at each heart beat increases with exercise.
3 Athlete A: cardiac output
  $=70\,bpm \times 70\,ml = 490\,ml/min.$
  Athlete B: (more efficient) cardiac output
  $= 90\,bpm \times 60\,ml = 540\,ml/min.$

15 Structure
1 Air passages, lungs and diaphragm
2 To filter air
3 To prevent food entering the lungs
4 Flexible strong tube made of rings of cartilage, known as the windpipe
5 Gases are exchanged in the alveoli of the lung tissue.

16 Breathing action
1 Intercostal muscles, between the ribs, pull the rib cage upwards when they contract which increases the thoracic space.
2 Oxygen and carbon dioxide are exchanged in the alveoli. Capillaries surrounding the alveoli allow these gases to pass to and from the bloodstream.

3 Minute volume = tidal volume × respiratory rate

17 Energy systems

1 Aerobic energy systems require oxygen; anaerobic systems work without a direct supply of oxygen.

2 Lactic acid reduces performance as muscles become painful and difficult to contract. Oxygen is needed to convert lactic acid back to pyruvic acid.

3 Aerobic – distance running, anaerobic – sprinting, aerobic and anaerobic – team games where running and sprinting occur

18 Types of skill

1 Positive – kicking a ball in rugby and soccer, negative – forward pass in rugby and basketball

2 OPEN – hockey dribble – tennis volley – tennis serve – springboard diving – CLOSED

3 a Starting gun in athletics, wind in sailing
b Somersault, high jump clearance

19 Practice and learning

1 a Shooting in netball, serving in table tennis (any continually repeated skill)
b Long-distance running, using heavy weights for training or in competition (any strenuous event)

2 Watching a demonstration because it is easy to see and copy actions, rather than a video or a picture.

3 Held in position by the coach, using a mechanical device such as a trampoline rig

20 Information processing

1 The brain can only process a limited amount of information at any one time.

2 Selective attention is the process by which the brain selects appropriate information from large amounts information.

3 Serve shuttle in badminton: decision – serve shuttle; output – produce service shot; feedback – did shuttle land in expected area?; input – information about way service was played; decision – alter service action to produce different end result.

21 Motivation

1 Taking part in the activity

2 Prize money, awards

3 Young children may take part in a sport for enjoyment, as they get older they may be motivated by awards or by money if they become professional.

22 Arousal and aggression

1 A long jumper might raise their arousal level before they run up by getting the crowd to clap. In shooting, low arousal levels are important so that the performer is calm.

2 Performers need to be assertive, forceful

3 When control is lost, performance declines and often leads to foul play, as in team sports.

23 Goal setting

1 System for target or goal setting –
S: specific; M: measurable; A: accepted; R: realistic; T: time; E: exciting; R: recorded

2 In long jumping – did the performer reach the required (measurable) distance?

3 R: realistic

24 Personality

1 Any two sportsmen or women involved in an individual sport.

2 Lots of movement, high levels of excitement, whole body activities – any sportsperson involved in a team sport

25 Body types

1 Gymnasts are likely to be of similar build, as are sumo wrestlers

2 a Meso/ecto: marathon runner/ gymnast
b Meso/endo: hammer thrower/ weight lifter

3 Rugby – backs are likely to be smaller than forwards, and there may be a variety of body shapes in the forwards.

26 Gender: physiology

1 Formula One motor racing, sumo wrestling

2 Triple jump, hammer throw, pole vault, 3000 m steeplechase

3 Mainly in racket games as in doubles matches in tennis or badminton

27 Clothing

1 New materials made into one-piece suits with slippery surfaces used in speed skating, cycling and swimming; waterproof breathable fabric for outdoor activities

2 Hard to prove, but one-piece suits may reduce drag and, therefore, could improve performance time in skating, cycling, etc.

3 Kevlar® is used extensively to provide protection in hockey and ice hockey, particularly for goalkeepers.

28 Facilities and sports surfaces

1 Can prevent rain, wind, frost affecting the game, keeps temperatures down in extremely hot weather

2 Football – ball bounces too high and players can be injured falling on hard surface

Answers

BBC GCSE Check and Test: Physical Education

3 High jump, pole vault, etc.

29 Equipment

1 Fibre glass vaulting poles, more aerodynamic javelins increase distance thrown

2 a Video analysis helps teachers and coaches improve technique and performance

b Spectators can see more with video replays on large screens, also miniature cameras attached to sportsmen or to equipment, such as inside cricket stumps

30 Health-related fitness

1 Fitness is a measure of the body's ability to complete activities for everyday life efficiently and effectively.

2 a Ability of the heart to pump blood and deliver oxygen where needed in the body

b Any event that is continuous, such as long-distance running, swimming, etc.

3 Legs in distance running, arms in distance swimming

4 Shoulder in javelin throwing, hips/groin – splits in gymnastics, back in high jump

31 Strength

a A high amount of force applied quickly – shot put, javelin throw, long and high jump

b Power is the combination of strength and speed.

c Rugby, static, pushing in a scrum; badminton, explosive, smash; gymnastics, explosive, somersault; swimming, dynamic, sprinting; netball, dynamic, moving around court; cricket, explosive, bowling

32 Skill-related fitness

1 Trampolining, skiing, basketball, volleyball, netball, etc.

2 Static balance – handstand or similar, dynamic balance – cycling, moving on a gymnastic beam

3 Simple reaction: starting gun in athletics, performer responds to one stimulus; choice reaction: playing a shot in tennis, performer has to respond to more than one stimulus (ball travelling over net and opponent's movement)

33 Cardiovascular fitness tests

1 Better levels of cardiovascular fitness shorten the time a person needs to recover after exercise, i.e. get back to his or her resting pulse rate.

2 Description of either Cooper 12 minute run or multi-stage fitness test as in topic 33

34 Strength tests

1 Muscular endurance is determined by how long a muscle or group of muscles can work. Therefore, to test this, performers have to repeat actions for as long as possible and score either the number of repetitions or the time taken before actions can no longer be performed, i.e. pull ups, sit ups, etc..

2 A broad jump may require more skill to perform correctly than a vertical jump, description of test procedure checked against topic 34

35 Flexibility and agility tests

1 Detailed description of the sit and reach test, check against topic 35

2 Any type of test with running and change of direction, but not as complicated as the Illinois test

36 Other fitness tests

1 Any kind of balance where movement is involved – cycling slowly, walking along a narrow beam, etc.

2 Kicking a ball against a wall with alternate feet, either on ground, in air or combination of both

37 Principles of training

1 Improve or maintain fitness levels and performance skills

2 Reversibility means that the body adapts to reduced training by a loss of fitness.

3 Overload can be achieved by increasing the frequency, intensity and duration of training sessions. Any application of these principles to a sport or activity

38 FITT and training zone

1 Any training sessions using frequency, intensity, time and type variations

2 a 200 beats/minute

b Safe max. heart rate reduces with age

3
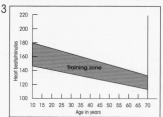

39 Seasonal planning

1 a Tennis, athletics, etc.

b Cricket in the summer and soccer in the winter

108

2 a Play a different sport

b Only take part in selected events with extended rest periods between competitions

40 Session planning

1 a Increases the blood flow to the muscles, stretches muscles and tendons, increases mental arousal

b to reduce blood pooling in the lower legs

2 Any activity where skill or fitness are subjected to repeated actions, e.g. a goalkeeper having to react to consecutive balls to left and right of goal, or a performer in netball receiving consecutive passes from a number of players

3 Passive opposition enables players and teams to establish specific skills and patterns of play in a simulated game situation without being tackled or losing possession of the ball.

41 Mental and anaerobic training

1 a Set personal goals and targets

b As above, but also about relationships with other team members

2 a Short bursts of high intensity activity – sprinting, run up for long jump or vault in gymnastics

b Heart walls grow stronger (esp. the left ventricle), lactic acid is dispersed more quickly enabling longer muscle action

42 Aerobics

1 a Using a platform to increase load by having to step up

b Water provides good resistance to activity, and buoyancy of water reduces weight on joints

2 a Heart becomes more efficient, stroke volume increases, recovery is quicker, blood volume increases, arteries grow larger

b Diaphragm becomes stronger, lungs expand more, alveoli become more efficient

43 Aerobic training

1 Oxygen debt is repaid during rest periods.

2 Athletics and swimming, distances above 30 metres and times above 30 seconds

3 Requires little equipment, training levels easily controlled by the performer; does not develop anaerobic fitness, difficult to accurately measure training amounts

44 Fartlek aerobic training

1 Speed play

2 Distance jogging and any extended activity for aerobic training, repeated short sprints for anaerobic training

3 Range of both aerobic and anaerobic training can be adapted for different sports, difficult to measure training amounts

45 Weight training

1 Safer and more comfortable to use, work specific muscle groups, amount of weight used can be easily adjusted

2 Use a light weight with a high number of repetitions

3 Isometric: very little if any movement, any activity using free or weights machine; isokinetic: moving weights so that the muscle length shortens, such as bicep curl

46 Circuit training

1 Any circuit showing a variety of skills, but similar skills should not be adjacent to each other

2 Press ups, pull ups, squat thrusts, astride jumps, sit ups, shuttle runs

3 Variety of activities help maintain motivation levels, adaptable for a variety of sports for fitness and skills, can be done with little specialist equipment, can accommodate a large number of people in a small area

47 Altitude training and plyometrics

1 The body increases the mass of red blood cells and haemoglobin. Therefore, after altitude training, athletes competing at sea level make more effective use of oxygen and can improve their performances.

2 Cost and availability

3 a Muscles are rapidly stretched and the natural elasticity of the muscle is used in rebounding

b Explosive strength

48 Flexibility training

1 Gymnastics: groin flexibility in splits and hurdling; javelin throwing: shoulder flexibility for greater force in the throw

2 Vigorous movement of limbs is essential in a good warm up, but coach must know the limits of the performer's stretching ability, otherwise, it could cause injury

3 Can stretch more thoroughly, but need to be careful as less control

49 Stimulants and analgesics

1 Caffeine

2 Ephedrine, dexedrine, etc. – suppress pain, increase confidence and alertness

3 Codeine – constipation, mental apathy, low blood pressure, etc.

Answers

BBC GCSE Check and Test: Physical Education

50 Anabolic agents

1 Testosterone – development of male characteristics (deep voice, chin hair, etc.)
2 a Increase in muscle growth and competitiveness
  b Any sports requiring power and endurance, i.e. shot putting, sprinting, rowing, etc.
3 Heart disease; high blood pressure; bone, tendon and ligament weakness; infertility; liver disorders; aggressive behaviour; etc.

51 Beta blockers, diuretics, peptide hormones and analogues

1 Shooting, snooker – beta blockers
2 To remove fluids and, therefore, reduce weight quickly – boxing, wrestling

52 Smoking and alcohol

1 Tar in the lungs makes them less efficient
2 Carbon monoxide reduces effectiveness of haemoglobin, lung cancer, less resistance to illness such as bronchitis, loss of smell and taste, etc.
3 Balance, dehydration, etc.

53 Food

1 Simple carbohydrates – sugars, jams, honey; complex carbohydrates – starches, vegetables, cereals, rice, pasta, bread
2 Glycogen, stored in the liver
3 Cholesterol is found in the blood, animal products contain cholesterol; can lead to clogging of the arteries

54 Balanced diet

1 A balance of different types of food – meat, vegetables, etc. to give a balance of protein, fat, carbohydrate, vitamins, minerals and fibre
2 Obesity – eating more than the body requires leads to a build up of excess fat; anorexia – a mental illness where insufficient food is consumed
3 Enhance flavour and colour

55 Diet and energy

1 Basal metabolic rate – lowest level of energy required for normal healthy living
2 Smaller body size
3 An office worker will not be as active as a 15-year-old male, so will require less energy.

56 Diet for sport

1 Carbohydrates are converted into glycogen which provides energy
2 Pasta has a high content of carbohydrate, which is essential for providing energy.
3 Help restore glycogen levels

57 Leisure time

1 Leisure time is non-working time.
2 Many people work part-time or flexitime, or work from home. This increases opportunities for leisure.
3 At work, more production lines are computer-controlled, requiring fewer people and less manual labour; at home, labour-saving appliances reduce time required to do chores – all factors in increasing the time available for leisure

58 Vocation

1 A professional is employed to play a sport. A semi–professional is paid for playing sport, but will also have another job which may not be related to any sporting activity.
2 Boxing, cricket, etc.
3 Football

59 Schools: the National Curriculum

1 To ensure that all pupils and students have similar experiences in physical education irrespective of where they live or what type of school they attend.
2 Athletics, swimming, games, dance, etc.
3 Schools have different facilities

60 School: examinations

1 Practical activities, theory of physical education and personal exercise plans
2 Short course GCSE, Certificate of Achievement and Junior Sports Leader Award and GNVQs
3 AS and A2 physical education exams which count towards University admission, students can take GNVQs in Leisure and Tourism and Sport and Recreation

61 Schools: extra-curricular activities and clubs

1 Activities which take place before/after school, during lunchtimes; not part of the normal physical education curriculum
2 Provide opportunities for talented students to improve at their events and play at higher levels in school, district, county and national competitions
3 Facilities of the school or college, interests of the teachers and students, etc.
4 Clubs can help with equipment, coaching; provide opportunities for students to take part in junior teams and competitions

62 Excellence and Sportsmarks

1 To put sport at the heart of weekly life in every school, to improve the provision of sports facilities, etc. – increases

110

opportunities for students to participate in sporting activities

2 Twelve opportunities for activity for all students, 35% of students taking part in extra-curricular activities, etc.

3 Not enough students taking part in extra-curricular activities

63 Sports Colleges

1 Students must gain a sports qualification such as GCSE P.E., time available for P.E. should be increased, links should be developed with sport governing bodies, school facilities should be expanded, etc.

2 Youth Sports Trust and the Department for Education and Skills

64 Access and age

1 Insufficient specialist facilities in their local area, e.g. few swimming pools have high diving boards

2 Golf, swimming, green bowling

3 Most invasion games involve contact, older people need longer to recover, muscles and joints are not as strong and may be damaged more easily

65 Ability and disability

1 To raise the profile of disabled in sport, to ensure that plans for sport include the disabled, to provide sporting opportunities for the disabled, to improve access to sport, etc.

2 Athletics, basketball

66 Gender

1 Difficult for women to commit time to sport if they have 'home' responsibilities, fewer role models for girls in sport

2 Two role models from any sport, e.g. Williams sisters in tennis, Paula Radcliffe in athletics, etc.

3 Less media coverage of women in sports means a lower profile, fewer women involved in the media

67 Family, ethnicity and friends

1 Provide money for clothes, transport children to events, etc.

2 Excluding people from playing a sport because of their race or ethnic background is racist.

3 Similar sporting interests or by not taking part at all

68 Tradition and culture

1 Rugby in Wales and New Zealand, cricket in India, Pakistan, ice hockey in Canada

2 Provide inspiration to children to take part in sports

3 Top level performers, known as Sporting Ambassadors, visit schools

4 By providing funds for facilities, by ensuring there is time for P.E. in schools, promoting sporting activity as beneficial to health

69 Sports councils

1 To provide UK world-class performers with world-class support, to extend the UK's profile and influence on the international sporting stage, to promote ethical standards and manage anti-doping programmes, to create a framework for attracting and running the worlds major sporting events

2 Sport England, Sport Scotland, The Sports Council for Wales, The Sports Council for Northern Ireland

3 More people involved, more places to play, more medals

70 Sports governing bodies

1 Rules, competitions, team selection, clubs and players, etc.

2 To encourage as many people as possible to participate in sport, to provide an organisation for all governing bodies of sport

3 Games and Sports, Major Spectator Sports, Movement and Dance, etc.

71 The BST and the YST

1 Junior Sports Leader Award, Community Sports Leader Award, Higher Sports Leader Award, Basic Expedition Leader Award

2 Fun and success in sport, sports suitable for children's own level, opportunities to develop a range of sporting skills, etc.

3 Training for students in schools and colleges to run TOP Festivals in primary schools

72 Sports club funding

1 Money paid by spectators to watch an event – players wages are very high in some sports and, even with full capacity, it may be insufficient to pay players

2 Replica strip, badges, books, balls, etc.

3 a Raise money through fundraising activities, pay a subscription fee, make a donation to help the club
b Work unpaid, cut grass, decorate and maintain club property, coach, etc.

73 Grants and the National Lottery

1 Through taxation, Department for Culture, Media and Sport

2 Through national government grants, council tax and revenue from sports facilities and sports centres

3 The National Lottery allocates 5.6 p for every £1.00 taken. In 2002, this amounted to £17 million every month.

74 Sport sponsorship

1 Equipment, coaching, financial help for training and competing, etc.

2 Team strips, help with transport to events

3 Many examples: Barclay – Premiership; Speedo – swimming; etc.

75 Sport sponsors

1 Sponsorship is powerful advertising, popular and televised sponsored events make brand names well known; sponsoring unsuccessful individuals, teams or events, company or product associated with a sport may not be appropriate, etc.

2 Increases their income and enables them to compete at the highest level

3 Sponsors may want to have control over a sport by deciding on which sportsmen and women can play, the rules and venues for events. Governing bodies may rely too heavily on sponsorship.

76 Media

1 In depth coverage with a lot of information, but old news

2 Stories about sports personalities that may have little to do with their sport

3 Rugby, cricket; gymnastics, archery, etc.

77 Television

1 Any situation that helps the referee to make the correct decision, e.g. video on the goal line in football, cameras in cricket stumps, etc.

2 Events arranged to suit best viewing times

3 Any event that takes place over a large area, e.g. golf, marathon, etc.

78 Local authority provision

1 Dual use: school hires out their facilities after school hours; joint provision: facilities shared by the school and the community

2 Might provide good facilities beyond school's or college's own finances

3 To provide sport and leisure facilities for the public

4 Financial support to reduce costs to the public

5 Playing fields, etc.

79 Private and commercial organisations

1 Often have swimming pools and fitness rooms for guests and make these available to the public through leisure clubs

2 Commercial sports club: often provide a facility which local authority may not be able to provide, e.g. golf club; voluntary sports clubs: usually run by their own members, e.g. amateur football club

3 Provide playing facilities, fields, changing rooms, team strips, help with travel, etc.

80 Sports clubs

1 To provide facilities and opportunities for its members to play the game and meet socially, to organise competitions and matches, to encourage people to take part in their sport, etc.

2 Chairman, vice-chairman, secretary, etc.

3 Raise profile and improve image of club

81 International events

1 Competition where individuals or teams from different countries compete against each other

2 Europa Cup (athletics), Cup of Nations (African football championships), etc.

3 Fastest, Highest, Stongest

82 Hosting international events

1 Cost, organisation, security, etc.

2 More and better sports facilities; access, transport and hotels improved; etc.

3 Finance needed to build new/to improve old facilities might be taken from areas such as education or healthcare

83 Olympics

1 With major sponsorship deals

2 Any event such as Hitler in Berlin 1936, USA not competing in Moscow 1980 or Soviet Union not competing in Los Angeles in 1984

3 Any competitor in a named sport with extended explanation, e.g. Jesse Owen, etc.

84 The UK Sports Institute

1 Expert advice, personal development and training, coaching, support staff, etc.

2 a Sailing
  b Mountaineering
  c Skiing
  d Outdoor activities

3 Bath University, Bedford, Gateshead, etc.

85 Amateur and professional

1 Professional, semi-professional and amateurs can compete in the same event

2 Earn money, travel the world, etc.